Marketing in B2B

Marketing in B2B

How Do SME Managers Make Decision?

Hairul Rizad and Abu Bakar

PARTRIDGE

A Penguin Random House Company

To order additional copies of this book, contact
Toll Free 800 101 2657 (Singapore)
Toll Free 1 800 81 7340 (Malaysia)
orders.singapore@partridgepublishing.com

www.partridgepublishing.com/singapore

CONTENTS

LIST OF TABLES

LIST OF FIGURES

LIST OF ABBREVIATIONS

ANOVA	-	Analysis of variance
DV	-	Dependent variable
IV	-	Independent variable
QUAN	-	Quantitative
QUAN	-	Quantitative
RO	-	Research Objective
RQ	-	Research Question
SME	-	Small Medium Enterprise
SPSS	-	Statistic Package for Science Social

LIST OF APPENDICES

CHAPTER 1

INTRODUCTION

1.0   Introduction

The marketing decision making process in SME warrants investigation because the high failure rate in this sector is associated with a poor marketing decisions making process and inadequate understandings of how SME decision makers currently make their marketing decisions (Ali & Nelson, 2006). Furthermore, there are limited number of studies that particularly investigate this issue in the context of Malaysia as far as the researcher is concerned.

1.1   Research background

Small and Medium-sized Enterprises (SMEs) have been recognised as one of the instruments of growth for many countries including Malaysia (Abu Bakar, 2003; Abdul Ghani, Yusniza, Apnizan & Syed Zambri, 2009; Norhazana, Eta & Elina, 2010). SMEs play vital roles in Malaysian development such as serving as a training ground for workers and entrepreneurs to develop their skills, curbing the monopoly power of larger firms, reducing country's vulnerability to financial crises, playing a complementary role with larger firms, as well as driving equitable income distribution (SMIDEC, 2009).

SMEs in Malaysia represent 97.3% of total business establishments (645,000) in the country, of which 80% of these SMEs are micro enterprises (business organisations with less than

5 full-time employees and RM300,000 annual sales turnover), and 86.5% of the SMEs are concentrated in the service sector (SMEs Census 2011, Department of Statistics). SMEs contribute 32.7% of Malaysia's gross domestic product (GDP), 57.4% of employment, and 19% of total export (Department of Statistics, Malaysia and SME Corporation Malaysia, 2013). Given their magnitude in Malaysian economy, development among SMEs has become a major economic agenda for the Malaysian Government and relevant policy makers. In view of their significance and potential, the Malaysian Government has given due recognition and has allocated significant amount of funds and resources to further enhance the growth of this sector. As such, various initiatives have been undertaken by government agencies such as Small and Medium Enterprise Corporation Malaysia (SME Corp. Malaysia), Ministry of Trade and Industry (MITI), and Malaysian Agricultural Research and Development Institute (MARDI) to drive the growth of this sector.

In spite of the priorities and efforts made by the government agencies, SME sector in this country continues to face numerous challenges as highlighted by the Asia-Pacific Economic Cooperation (APEC, 1994), Small and Medium Industries Development Corporation (SMIDEC, 2002), Ting (2004), United Parcel Services (UPS) survey (2005), and Ali and Nelson (2006). These challenges include lack of access to loans, limited adoption of technology, lack of human resources, competition from MNCs, and globalisation. Most recently, a survey by Malaysia External Trade Development Corporation (MATRADE, 2007) revealed that SMEs in Malaysia still inherit limited marketing and promotion strategies. Lack of marketing is one of the most important factors affecting the growth of many SME businesses (Brush *et al.*, 2009; Elin & Leon, 2010). World Bank (2006) identified that lack of marketing knowledge and strategies is one of the main constraints for SMEs in Association of Southeast Asian Nations (ASEAN) to grow. Ali and Nelson (2006) further mentioned that inadequate understanding of how SMEs currently make their marketing decisions has contributed to the poor marketing decision making process and led to the unsatisfactory performance.

In Malaysia, marketing is one of the key elements in determining the success of SME businesses (Indarti & Langenberg, 2004; Bank Negara, 2006). The research conducted by Hashim (1999) on the problems faced by SMEs in Malaysia found that the most dominant problems faced by SMEs were related to sales and marketing, which accounted for 22% of all problems investigated in the study. This finding has also been confirmed by Hashim and Wafa (2002) and Muhammad *et al.* (2010). SME marketing capabilities remain a weak point in business management among SMEs. Most SMEs may understand the need to properly market and promote their products and services, but only few of them have the appropriate insights into the process of how to go about achieving it (SME Corp, 2006).

In response to weaknesses in marketing among SMEs, there has been a move to enhance marketing support programmes with assistance from the government agencies in areas including direct promotional activities, brand and franchise development, and linkages with large companies. With a more effective mechanism in place, the Government hopes that the SMEs' contribution to total exports will increase from the current estimate of about 19% to 30%. Programme like MITI's Industrial Linkage Programme (ILP) aims to develop domestic SMEs into competitive manufacturers and suppliers to multinational corporations (MNCs) and large scale industries, and to provide assistance to those with the potential but are lacking in certain areas such as quality certification and processing efficiency. However, extensive involvement of the Government in SME development has created high dependency of SMEs towards the Government in formulating the strategy to access new markets, to increase their revenue, and to expand their customer base. This policy has indirectly discouraged SMEs from searching for new potential customers so as to keep their business growing. Thus, SMEs should not focus only on providing those products and services for existing customers, but also by providing products and services whenever the customers need those products and services (Sanders, 2005). This situation may perhaps provide an insight into why the SMEs in Malaysia prefer to "stay small" in business (Hazlina & Shen, 2009).

Moreover, the contribution to business failure rate due to weakness in marketing capability for Malaysian SMEs is estimated to be 60% (Norhazlina & Pi, 2009). Therefore, this study was conducted in an attempt to explore this issue and to formulate a workable framework for the SMEs to enhance their marketing decision making process, which is deemed as the major challenge that hinders their growth and development.

1.2 Conceptual Issues in SME Business to Business Marketing Decision Making Process Research

The following terms, which are an inherent part of the title of the dissertation, are discussed in more detail to provide greater clarity to the research design.

1.2.1 SME definition

SMEs can be defined in various ways, but generally it is classified according to the socioeconomic development of each country (Tahir, Mohamad, & Hasan, 2011). Despite these non-standardised definitions, SMEs across the globe share certain common characteristics that differentiate them from large local firms or multinational corporations (MNCs). Like other countries, the Malaysian SMEs sector has attracted various definitions from different legitimate bodies such as the Coordinating Council for Development of Small-Scale Industries (CCDSI), the Ministry of International Trade and Industry (MITI), the Credit Guarantee Corporation (CGC), the Small and Medium-Sized Industry Development Corporation (SMIDEC), and the Ministry of Finance (Hashim, 2005). Each authority sets its own requirements for defining the SMEs based on a range of fixed indexes such as number of workers, sales volume, capital employed, and asset value in order to accomplish specific objectives in certain programmes.

The wide definitional gap reveals the inadequacy of Malaysian Government in understanding the nature of SMEs, thus creating confusions, administrative problems, and unequal financial opportunities to different types of SMEs across the industries. Hence, the National SME Development Council (NSDC), which is the highest policy-making body that comprises the Prime Minister as the Chairman, 15 ministers, the Governor of Malaysia National Bank, the Director-General of the Economic Planning Unit, and the CEO of the Multimedia Development Corporation has approved a unified definition of SMEs in Malaysia to be commonly used by all government ministries, agencies, and financial institutions for formulation and implementation of their respective SME development programmes in all sectors effective 9th June 2005. This standard definition ensures an objective, unequivocal classification of Malaysian SMEs based on two quantitative criteria namely number of employees or and annual sales turnover to facilitate the identification of SMEs in the various sectors and subsectors. The standard also helps Malaysia to formulate effective development policies, support programmes as well as provision of technical and financial assistance.

In 1st January 2014, a new SME definition was announced. The definition required high sales turnover to be classified for a profit-gaining organisation to be classified as a small or medium enterprise, in addition to the existing definition. For example, an SME in services sector needs to have only RM1 million annual sales turnover to qualify as a medium enterprise according to the old definition of SME up to 31st December 2013. However, with the new definition of SME in place, RM3 million annual sales turnover is required for a profit-gaining organisation to be classified as a medium enterprise. The new definition is expected to result in more firms being classified as SMEs, particularly from the services sector. This new definition will facilitate the country's transformation to a high-income nation through the initiatives under the SME Master Plan. As a result of the change in definition, the share of SMEs to total establishments is expected to increase from 97.3% currently to 98.5%. Table 1.1 summarises how micro, small, and medium enterprises are classified by the approved new definition of SME of the National SME Development Council (NSDC) using number of employees or annual sales turnover for four major sectors.

The categorisation of an SME entity into micro, small, and medium is not only benefitting the government and policy maker. It is also being acknowledged by the researchers in helping them to be specific in their study. For example, the characteristic of being "more reluctant to take risks" (MacGregor & Vrazalic 2005, p.513; Craige, 2013) is one which can be found in all sizes of entity, from micro to large.

Table 1.1: New SME Definition Based on Size

Category	Micro	Small	Medium
Manufacturing	Sales turnover of less than RM300,000 OR employees of less than 5	Sales turnover from RM300,000 to less than RM15 mil OR employees from 5 to less than 75	Sales turnover from RM15 mil to not exceeding RM50 mil OR employees from75 to not exceeding 200
Services and other sectors	Sales turnover of less than RM300,000 OR employees of less than 5	Sales turnover from RM300,000 to less than RM15 mil OR employees from5 to less than 30	Sales turnover from RM3 mil to not exceeding RM20 mil OR employees from 30 to not exceeding 75

Source: SME Corporation, 2014.

1.2.2 Marketing decision making process

Marketing decision making processes in SME has been acknowledged by many researchers (Coviello *et al.*, 2000; Gilmore *et al.*, 2001; Hill, 2001; Reijonen, 2010; Sarah, 2012). In large organisations, decision making process is structured and routine and involves several steps that include refinement of the alternatives. Therefore, time scales are long and need planning. Sometimes, large organisations have problems where various parts of the organisation do not know what the others are doing (Blois, 2000). In SMEs, marketing decisions are made by the owner-manager, who is involved in all aspects of company activities. She or he does not need structures and framework, but will intuitively and very quickly make the decisions based on previous experience and common sense (Chaston, 2000; Tamara, 2010). Decisions are sometimes made in an even haphazard, informal, spontaneous, or unstructured way (Mike *et al.*, 2006; Gilmore, Joensuu, 2009; Reijonen, 2010; Tamara, 2010).

According to Walsh and Lipinski (2009), marketing in SMEs is not as well developed or influential as it is in large firms. Large organisations are often large enough to have a marketing department that permits the delineation of functions and activities. This difference can be attributed to certain limitations that SMEs face including limited resources in terms of finance, time, and marketing knowledge (Gilmore *et al.*, 2001; Reijonen, 2010). Many researchers agree that no theories may be considered inappropriate to explain the marketing decision making process within SMEs (Sarah, 2012). It is argued that SME owner-managers tend to view marketing narrowly and consider marketing the same as selling or advertising (Reijonen, 2010).

1.2.3 Business-to-business relationship

Before we examine the extant literature on SME marketing decision making, it is important for us to understand the context of decision making phenomenon within SMEs business-to-business relationship. Marketing decision making refers to those marketing-related decisions of significant importance to the firm in terms of business and financial performance, long-term survival, and the significant impacts they have upon all or most of the other functional areas of the business relationship (Jocumsen, 2002). The following section presents a high-level overview of my knowledge about business-to-business relationships as it relates to the marketing decision making process framework proposed in this research.

In business-to-business relationship process, SMEs must define their purpose for engaging in relationship, select parties for relationship, and develop marketing programme for the relationship. According to Sheth & Parvatiyar (1995), such relationship has potential to improve marketing productivity and to create mutual values between a firm and its customer by increasing marketing effectiveness or improving marketing efficiencies. It can be understood in this context that business-to-business relationship is a process that includes attracting, maintaining, and enhancing relationship between firms (Berry, 1983; Dwyer, 1987). Attracting new customers should be viewed only as an intermediate step in the marketing process, while developing closer relations with the customers and making them loyal are equally important aspects of marketing. The focuses here are to secure and maintain a long-term relationship between firms and to lead a greater firm profitability and customer loyalty (Kotler, 2000).

In general, many thought that business-to-business relationship shares the same condition with other marketing relationship unions such as business-to-customer relationship and customer service relationship. However, business engaged in relationship marketing activities focus to achieve competitive advantage, while consumers engaged in relationship marketing activities are to simplify their involvement in the marketing process and service organisation engaged in relationship marketing activities are to improve the quality and satisfaction of service in the market process. Thus, there are differences in the goals and practices of marketing across each of these areas.

In business-to-business (B2B) relationship, buyers do not consume the products or services themselves. It is different in business-to-consumer (B2C) relationship where products and services are consumed personally by the people who buy them (Fill & Fill, 2005). In B2B, many SMEs have successes in selling their products and services as they have built the long-term relationships with clients who stay loyal. This finding is confirmed by Ford *et al.* (2002) and Hallin *et al.* (2006), and Laura (2011) that the most important aspect in a B2B world is relationship. Relationship is the centre of all activities directed towards establishing, developing, and maintaining successful exchange with customers and other components. The development and maintenance of positive relationships between buying and selling organisations are pivotal to success. Collaboration and partnership over the development, supply, and support of products and services are considered core elements of B2B. A well-developed ability to create and sustain successful working relationship with customers gives the SMEs a significant competitive advantage.

1.3   Problem Statement

Decision making is a crucial aspect of managing performance within the SMEs as practitioners are oftentimes in fire-fighting mode in order to deal with a myriad of problems and opportunities that present themselves in rapid succession. Decisions can vary from the strategic or tactical, to a multitude of everyday operational decisions, which are often unsupported by relevant information and are under serve time pressure. As a result, decision makers are frequently pressured into making suboptimum decisions in order to deal with one crisis and get onto another, often with little thought to their general impact or contribution to be overall performance of the enterprise. Commercial applications have failed to adequately provide a coherent method for operational decisions in this environment, in spite of a more comprehensive effort in the past number of years.

The context of making decision in SMEs is different from the context of making decision in large companies because (1) SMEs owner-managers do not have access to solid information like the managers of large companies, (2) SMEs owner-managers are confronted with a more hostile external environment (which sometime is considered insignificant for a large company), and (3) SMEs owner-managers are confronted with repetitive decisions compared to the large companies that often develop routines to manage and make effective use of the managers' time in their managerial activities. On the other hand, decisions made by SMEs owner-managers are assumed to be more responsive based on specific issues and as a result of being reluctant in adoption of market orientation (Mohammed, 2011) that forms the basis of decision making characteristic in SME organisation.

The finding on lack of adoption of market orientation among SMEs owner-managers has been supported by recent researches (e.g., Mohammed, 2011; Alberto & Gianluigi, 2012). In reality, the dimension of market orientation may not be applicable in the SME sector. Several key factors inhibit the ability of small businesses in focusing the market orientation that includes unclear view of the customer requirement, commitment with the status quo, lack of competitive differentiation, limited resources, short-term focus, and perception that marketing as not important to organisation performance. In particular, the SME owner-managers are usually the sole decision makers who decide to adopt (or not) marketing approach. They rely on what they think what marketing is and their expectancies about the consequences of the adoption of such an approach in their organisations. This notion means that it is evaluated subjectively, i.e., according to the SME owner-managers' perceptions about marketing. This is in line with the finding of previous researchers (e.g., Becherer, Halstead & Haynes 2003; Carson & Gilmore 2000) who stressed the influence of the inherent characteristics of SMEs owner-manager in the choice to adopt (or not) such an approach. This notion means that conservative SME owner-manager are likely to reject the adoption of the marketing approach in their organisations as it would represent an innovation in itself and, as such, may be perceived as too risky (Marcati, Guido & Peluso 2006). In fact, whilst marketing decision-making processes in the large organisations tend to be formal and highly structured, in SMEs, such processes tend to be simple, informal, instinctive, and different from the theoretical models developed in the literature. Most researchers refer this as an entrepreneurial marketing, which is intuitive and situation-specific in nature, as well as its implementation without a pre-planning activity.

In SMEs operations, the owner-manager is often one of the top managers and participates in the decision-making process on daily basis (Miller & Besser, 2005). The owner-manager of the SMEs has a more direct effect on the decision-making process than the CEO of a large corporation (Payne *et al.*, 2005). Generally, the owner-manager has the final word on business decisions and selects the inputs that he or she will accept on each decision (Payne *et al.*, 2005). As the owner-manager has a direct control of the SMEs business operations, the influences on a single decision-maker appear to be more directly significant to the business (Feltham *et al.*, 2005: Gibcus *et al.*, 2009; Richard, 2013). The reason is simple. While owners of larger organisation employ professional managers, most SMEs owner-managers prefer to manage their firm by themselves. There are several articles directly related to the SMEs owner-managers (McGraw & Roger, 2001; Walker & Brown, 2004; Ho, 2011; Mahmood & Hanafi, 2012; Rocha, de Mello, Pacheco, de Abreu Farias, 2012; Nielsen & Nielsen, 2010; Gray & McNaughton, 2010; Donald, 2010; Richard, 2013), stating that demographic factors such as age, gender, ethnicity and education have a considerable impact on SMEs owner-managers' decision process. Therefore, it would seem reasonable to investigate the demographic profile of SMEs owner-managers that form the fundamental dimensions of this study.

Decision-makers in all businesses are influenced by a variety of factors (Turner, 2002). These factors do not necessarily have a direct influence on the outcomes of decisions, but may instead act on the information that is being fed into the process (Kieren, 2007). These factors can be grouped into two categories namely information sources (Varis & Littunen, 2010; Cacciolatti *et al.*, 2011; M. Krishna Moorthy, Annie, Carolineoo, Chang Sue Wei, Jonathan Tan Yong Ping, & Tan Kah Leong, 2012) and driving factor (Elaine, 2007; Lee, 2012 Collis, 2010; Kristina, 2012 O. Dwyer, 2010; Uma & Bhuvanes, 2011). These factors motivate the decision makers throughout the process. These factors may be prioritised differently by different managers (McDevitt, 2007). The general problem considered in this study was that decision makers in SME may identify and prioritise the factors differently from managers in large organisations. Therefore, it would seem reasonable to identify these factors and how it they impact throughout the decision process.

Effective decision making process requires more than knowledge of facts, concepts, and relationships (Schoemaker & Russo, 1993). Good decision making process also requires an organisation to constantly refine the knowledge gained from previous decisions (Ireland & Miller, 2004). Previous research found that failure to make right decision may have costly consequences to SMEs (Ireland & Miller, 2004). To make good decisions, SME decision makers often obtain information from multiple sources (McGee & Sawyer, 2003). Only then they would be able to process and translate the information into action. It is well accepted by many researchers that the decision process adapted by the SMEs owner-managers is often informal and based on personal and business priorities at any given point in time (Gilmore *et al.*, 2001). This argument, however, has been challenged by recent research that SMEs owner-managers do practise a structured process in their decision making process (Marwan, 2010; Jocumsen, 2004). The difference in view especially in the context of Malaysian SMEs was investigated in this study.

1.4   Research Objectives

The main purpose of this study was to investigate the process of marketing decision making among the Malaysian SMEs. The objectives of this study were to accomplish the following:

1. To identify and examine the influence of driving factors throughout decision making process.
2. To identify and examine sources of information in the process of making marketing decision.
3. To identify and examine decision making method used by the Malaysian SMEs.
4. To analyse the relationship between decision making method and decision outcomes.

1.5   Research Questions

To achieve the objectives above, the formulated research questions for this study are as follows:

1. What are the driving factors considered in the decision making process? Do these factors (driving factors) significantly influence the decision outcome?
2. What are the sources of information considered in making a decision for marketing? Are there any significant differences in adoption on sources of information based on the decision maker's characteristic (gender, age, ethnicity, and education level)?
3. What is the decision making method used in making marketing decision? Are there any significant differences in the adoption of decision method based on the decision maker's characteristic (gender, age, ethnicity, and education level)?
4. Are there any significant relationships between the adoption of decision making method and the decision outcome?

1.6 Research Scope

To provide a comprehensive basis for analysis, this study was done based on the data collected both qualitatively and quantitatively. The qualitative data were obtained from interviews with SME decision makers, while the quantitative data were obtained from respondents responsible in making decision in SMEs. To comply with ethics procedure, all the respondents were over 18 years of age. This study focused only on respondents accountable for making marketing decision.

The primary source of this study was generated through semistructured qualitative interviews. The interviews were conducted with randomly selected SMEs owner-managers to form a basis of the survey instrument for larger survey. These interviews were complemented by a survey questionnaire distributed to 500 respondents extracted from SME business directory. These respondents were randomly selected from various sectors registered under SME Corp. The respondents mainly came from Johor, Melaka, Negeri Sembilan, and Kuala Lumpur representing six industries namely building and construction, transportation, manufacturing, trading, electronic, and automotive. The combination of the interviews with the survey questionnaire would enhance the outcome of the study.

1.7 Significance of the Study

Most researchers agree that no general theory is accepted to explain the process of SME marketing decision. Instead, theory derived from large organisation is used to illustrate the current process. Consequently, there is still a big gap in knowledge on the issues associated with the process of making marketing decision in SMEs. It is the intention of this study to fill in the gap and to contribute to a better understanding on the process of SMEs marketing decision and on the issue that is widely debated but scarcely researched on.

It is also noticed that many researches concerning SMEs marketing decision are done not by Malaysian researchers. Thus, their research settings and recommendations might not be suitable in the context of Malaysia. Therefore, it is a privilege to undertake this research that takes cognizance of the biases.

In addition, this study can be used by other interested researchers to be compared and contrasted with the difficulties experienced by other countries in developing their SMEs. It is also hoped that the knowledge and the insights gained from this study can be used by other researchers as a basis for them to come out with a generalised theory in SMEs marketing process.

Finally, the findings of this study can be used as valuable inputs for the policy makers in Malaysia to come out with more effective strategies. These inputs are aimed to develop the SMEs competencies in marketing process and to provide reference in Malaysian SMEs research.

1.8   Outline of the Thesis

This thesis is organised into six chapters. Chapter 1 is concerned with a general overview and introduction to the focus of this study, the importance of the study, the background to the research, the research problem, and the contribution that the study makes to knowledge.

Chapter 2 reviews the literature on SMEs marketing decision making process. The review is split into two parts. Part one is the literature review on managerial decision making process. Part two discusses specifically the literature review on SMEs marketing decision making process and reviews the theoretical models relevant to this present study, besides providing the research framework.

Chapter 3 presents the research design and methodology for testing the hypotheses and investigating stages of the proposed model. The first part presents the qualitative research design and methodology including the interview questionnaire structure, pre-test of the questionnaire, sampling, data collection techniques, and data analysis techniques. The second part presents the quantitative research design and methods including the survey questionnaire structure, the measuring scales used, the pre-test and pilot test of the questionnaire, sampling techniques, data collection, and the statistical analysis plan.

Chapter 4 presents the results of the qualitative interviews with four SMEs decision makers. Descriptive data analysis and cross case analysis are used to report the results from the interviews.

Chapter 5 presents the results of the quantitative survey completed by all respondents using descriptive and inferential analysis. The discussion on the null hypotheses is also presented in this chapter.

Chapter 6 presents the similarities and differences from the results drawn from both qualitative and quantitative analyses. The discussion includes comparison of the implications of the findings from the interviews with four SMEs decision makers with the findings of the survey from 182 respondents. The results presented are integrated in terms of research framework, theoretical framework, and the four research questions. Finally, summary of the results, major findings, and the implications of these findings are presented. This chapter also provides a discussion on the limitations and gaps in this study, along with challenges for future research.

1.9   Summary

This chapter has presented the background of this research, research problem, research objectives, and significance and scope of the study, as well as the structure of the seven chapters in this thesis. The next chapter presents a literature review relating to SMEs marketing decision making process.

CHAPTER 2

LITERATURE REVIEW

2.0   Introduction

This chapter reviews literature and research that provide the background for the empirical investigation of the SMEs marketing decision making process. In the first part of this chapter, the managerial and organisational decision making overview is addressed through the concepts of organisational and individual decision making, and through the terminologies including decision, decision making, and the decision process. The assumptions of two leading theoretical approaches namely rational and behaviour theories are also discussed.

In the second part of this chapter, literature in marketing decision making process in SMEs is analysed by highlighting issue related to the process. Next, theoretical approaches and hypotheses in making the marketing decision are discussed. Finally, the chapter conclusion is presented.

2.1   Part 1: Research on Managerial Decision making

This section commences by defining the term "decision" and then reviews the process of decision making in organisations and the environment in which these decisions are made. Next, this section reviews the various models of managerial decision making.

2.1.1 Terminology of managerial decision, decision making, and decision process

The term "decision" has attracted the attention of many researchers in the managerial decision making literature. As a result, there have been many definitions to demonstrate the meaning of the term. For instance, decision is defined as an ongoing process of evaluating alternative for meeting the objective (Harrison, 1999), situation-behaviour combinations consisting of alternatives, uncertain events, and consequences (Hastlie, 2001), and choice of alternative (Robbins, 2003).

The term "decision making" has been defined in similar manner by previous authors and all researchers have established a common terminology that describes "decision making" as "a process of selection of one alternative among others" (Buhler, 2001).

Mintzberg *et al.* (1976) defined the decision processes as a set of action and dynamic factors that begins with the identification of stimulus for action and ends with specific commitment to action. Saimon (1977) described the decision-making process as a comprehensive process of recognition of decision occasions and possible courses of action, and consequently selection between the courses of action and the selected choice. Einhorn and Hogarth (1981) described that decision making process consists of three inter-related tasks namely information acquisition, evaluation, and feedback or learning, which form as a basis for the basic decision making model as depicted in Figure 2.1.

Figure 2.1: Basic decision making model

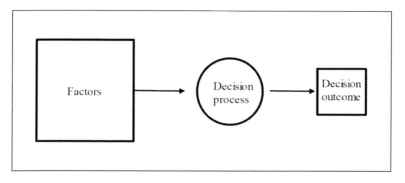

Source: Adapted from Einhorn & Hogarth (1981).

2.1.2 Conditions of Decision Making

Decision makers in any organisation often confront with three types of decision situations that are critical in making decision: certainty, uncertainty, and risk (Robbins, 2003). Hence, it is crucial for decision makers to thoroughly understand and carefully analyse the characteristics and the nature of the decision situations to arrive at good decisions. The failure in selecting a proper decision making framework surely would affect the organisation's success (Elliot, 1989).

Certainty is a situation wherein the decision maker can make precise determination because the outcome of every decision alternative is predictable and recognised, and there is no anticipated and associated threat or uncertain consequences (Marwan, 2010). Although this decision condition is not a characteristic of most managerial decision situation, it is usually associated with the routine decision situations that are more idealistic than realistic (Robbins, 2003). On the other hand, SME owner managers are constantly faced with decisions that have to be made under varying degrees of uncertainty. Therefore, the role of SME owner managers is to manage uncertainties by understanding the relationship between the risk and the opportunities in each business proposal (Olafsson, 2003).

The uncertain decision situation occurs when there is more than one possible outcome for each decision alternative, and the probabilities of these outcomes are unknown and unpredictable (Goodwin and Wright, 1991). Decisions under a degree of uncertainty rely on subjectivity, incomplete information, and personal preference for the consequences of outcomes (Baird, 1989). Uncertainty was defined as the variance between the processed information and the information required for completing an assignment (Marwan, 2010). Furthermore, uncertainty can be viewed as a firm's obstacle and challenge. Therefore, making decision in uncertain situation will result in many difficulties in estimating the degree of effectiveness of the decision. Nevertheless, uncertainty can be minimised throughout the decision making process, especially when a decision maker has a predetermined framework to analyse in certain situation and establish a clear decision procedures (Bhaskar, 2004).

The term "risk" is used to describe the probability of undesirable outcome (McKee, 2004). In other words, the main difference between risk and uncertainty is that, in risky situations, there is more than one possible outcome and the likelihood of each outcome can be known and predicted once a particular alternative is chosen. In the case of uncertainty, the decision maker cannot estimate the likelihood of certain outcomes for a selected alternative and therefore the likelihood of each outcome tends to remain unknown and unpredictable (Shapira, 1994).

In summary, the most imperative managerial decisions are burdened with risk and uncertainty, and these decision circumstances affect the quality of the decision outcome and accordingly, the overall performance of the organisation. Therefore, decisions made under risk and uncertainties have long-term consequences on the organisation (Marwan, 2010). As a result, risk and uncertainty are instrumental in determining the most appropriate decision making process to pursue in order to achieve a good effective decision.

2.1.3 Type of managerial decisions

It is important to stress the understanding of the types and characteristics of managerial decision in order to determine different decision making approaches used to resolve the decision problem (Simon, 1977). According to Simon (1977), there are two main types of decisions faced by manager. First, structured decisions are made to decide on repetitive problems and routine, proven set of steps, and planned procedures that have been established for making such decision to reach an optimal solution for the structured problem. Secondly, unstructured decisions, which are described as new or unique problems. Hence, decision problems are considered uncertain (Mintzerbg et al., 1976). Adopted from Harrison (1999), Table 2.1 shows the types of managerial decisions and describes each type in terms of dimension-classification, structure and strategy. The table also discusses the major difference among the types of managerial decisions.

Neuman and Hadass (1980) classified managerial decision making process into two categories. Firstly, the structure of decision making process, which is algorithmic (logical, quantitative, explicit and completely defined) and all decision choices and outcomes are recognised and quantitatively defined. Secondly, the unstructured decision making process, which is heuristic (experiential) and not all decision variables can be identified or measured. Unstructured decisions are made under conditions of uncertainty and high risk; the selected alternative is optimal and there is no best approach to making such a decision.

Cyert et al. (1956) identified three types of decision. First, a structured decision in which all the steps and procedures in the decision making process are prescribed. Second, an unstructured decision in which all the steps and procedures in the decision making process lack formal organisation. Third, a semi-structured decision in which steps and procedures in the decision making process are partly structured and partly unstructured.

Table 2.1: Types of managerial decisions

	Structured Decisions	Unstructured Decisions
Classification	• Programmable, routine, generic, computational, negotiated, compromise	• Nonprogrammable, unique, judgment, creative, adaptive, innovative, inspiration
Structure	• Procedure, predictable, certainty regarding cause/effect relationship recurring, within existing technologies, well defined information channels, definite decision criteria, outcome preference may be certain or uncertain	• Novel, unstructured, consequential, elusive and complex, uncertain cause / effect relationship, nonrecurring, information channels undefined, incomplete information, decision criteria may be unknown, outcome preference may be certain or uncertain
Strategy	• Reliance upon rules and principle, habitual reactions, prefabricated, response, uniform processing, computational techniques, accepted method for handling	• Reliance on judgment intuition and creativity, individual processing, heuristics problem-solving techniques, rules of thumb, general problem solving process

Source: Adapted from Harrison (1999, p.21)

2.2   Theoretical Approach on Decision Making

It has been suggested that decision making theories can be classified into two principles. Firstly, the normative or perspective approach that prescribes methods for making optimal decisions and describes how decisions should be made. Secondly, the descriptive approach, which concerns on the bounded way in which decisions are made in reality (Marwan, 2010).

The first decision theory that is widely known is rational decision theory or economic decision theory. The second theory is the behavioural decision theory, which is also known as descriptive theory. The assumptions of each theory are discussed in details in the next section.

2.2.1   Rational Decision Theory

The rational or economic decision theory is the first decision theory introduced in the managerial decision making literature. The theory is described as the quantitative method of decision making developed by mathematics and economics theorist. The mathematicians were mainly concerned with developing a mathematical theory of rational decision making whereas economic scholars were heavily concerned with alternative that should be made to maximise profits or utility. Moreover, the rational decision theory adopts a perspective approach rather than a descriptive approach. In other words, it describes how a decision should be made rather than how decisions are made in reality (Marwan 2010).

The theory assumes that the decision makers have acquired all the knowledge relevant to the decision. It suggests that the decision makers thoughtfully define the problem and determine their own preferences as represented in numerical terms of the value of payoff or utility of a given set of alternatives. Another assumption is that the decision makers gather information about the specified alternative courses of actions, consider the possible outcomes of each alternative, determine the relative likelihood of occurrences evaluates, rank all outcomes according to the predetermined preferences, and finally select the optimal alternative that has the maximum payoff. The assumptions of the rational decision theory are illustrated in Figure 2.2

In real practice, the decision makers' behaviour is somewhat different. They do not only simplify their information gathering; they also evaluate decision alternatives based on a simplified payoff function. The payoff function leads to alternatives being chosen not because they are necessarily the best, but because they have crossed some acceptable level or threshold (Kieren, 2007). Mintzberg and Westley (2001) described that rational decision theory is useful when the issues are clear, the data are reliable, the context is structured, thinking is clearly identifiable, and discipline can be applied.

In the context of SMEs managerial decision making, it is impossible for a decision maker to access all the information regarding a particular problem. This is due to the characteristic of SMEs environment that confronts with a more hostile external environment compared to large organisation. As cited in many researches, the decision making in SMEs is a complex process and is always burdened with risk and uncertainty. Thus, the underlying assumption and ideologies in the rational model are unlikely to be presented in SMEs environment.

Figure 2.2: Assumptions of the rational decision theory

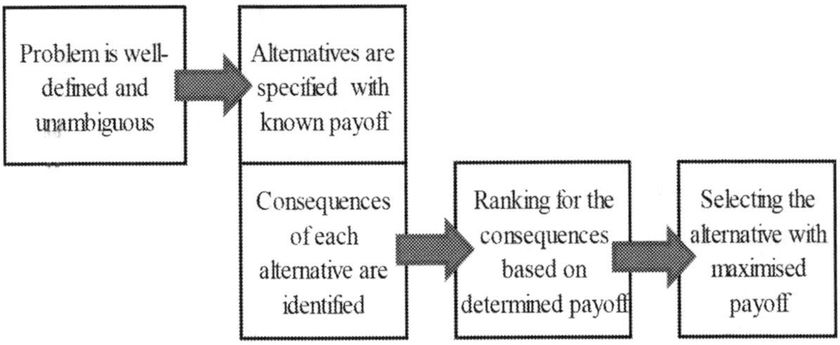

Source: Marwan (2010, p.16)

2.2.2 Behavioural Decision Theory

In spite of the fact that the rational decision approach is fundamental to serve economic models and theories, many researchers did not accept this approach for managerial decision-making (Shoa, 2006). They have criticised and challenged the assumptions of the economic rational school of thought from different angles. Consequently, this has led to the emergence of the behavioural decision school. They criticised the economic rational decision process and identified other important components that are missing from the economic model described as follows:

1. Alternatives are not generally "given" but should be sought, hence it is essential to include the search for alternatives as an important part of the process.
2. The information as to what consequences are attached to which alternatives is rarely "given" but the search for consequences is another important segment of the decision-making task.
3. The evaluation for alternatives is not usually made in terms of one clear, single, criterion-like profit. However, there are other intangible criteria that need to be considered also, thus making an evaluation based on "profit" is difficult, if not impossible. Instead of searching for the best alternative, the decision-maker is usually concerned with finding a satisfactory alternative – one that will achieve a specified goal and at the same time satisfy a number of assisting conditions.
4. In the real world, it is rare that the problem itself is "given" and well-defined, but exploring significant problems that an organisation should consider is an important organisation task.

In this theory, the managerial objectives are well-defined and the decision maker collects information about these objectives from various environmental sources. The collected, specified information within the organisation is used to identify a set of appropriate alternative to make a satisfactory choice. But, the amount of information and the consequent number of alternative are bounded by the lack of complete information, inevitable time and cost constraint, and the cognitive limitation of the decision maker (Harrison, 2000). Thus, the decision maker should consider these constraints because they significantly affect organisation strategies decision (Marwan, 2010, p.16). The assumptions of the behavioural decision theory are shown in Figure 2.3.

The behavioural theory assumes that the decision maker is a human being who has a limited knowledge about the possible alternatives and criteria, and is constrained by time, cost, and cognitive limitations. Thus, one is certainly not capable to accurately estimate the optimal choice from the available information and, consequently, to select the best or optimal alternative with maximised payoffs as assumed in the rational maximising behaviour. Similar to the SME context, the decision maker also face a limitation throughout the process due to constrain to access or use the information found in the complex real world. The restrictions on what information is available acknowledges that it may be impossible to examine all alternatives in all environmental states, so only a selection of the most probable occurs. This probably illustrated the behavioural approach to decision making for SME.

Figure 2.3: Assumption of the behaviour theory

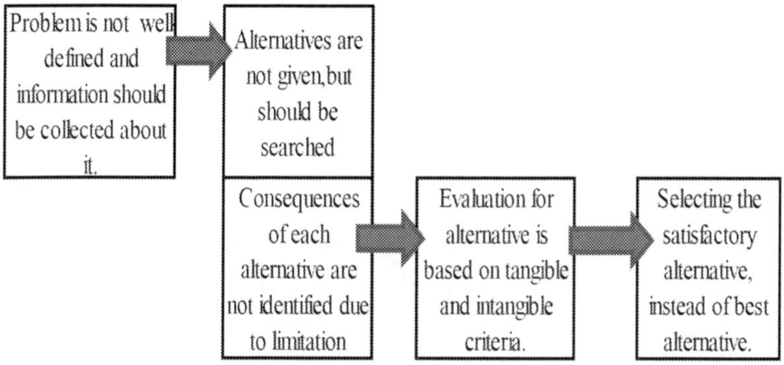

Problem is not well defined and information should be collected about it.	→	Alternatives are not given, but should be searched

Consequences of each alternative are not identified due to limitation	→	Evaluation for alternative is based on tangible and intangible criteria.	→	Selecting the satisfactory alternative, instead of best alternative.

Source: Marwan (2010, p.19)

2.3   Part II: SMEs marketing decision making

2.3.1   Marketing in SMEs

Marketing is regarded as relevant to both large and small organisations, and basic marketing principles are seen to apply to both (Reynolds, 2002; Siu and Kirby 1998). At the same time, it is recognised that SMEs marketing has unique characteristics that differentiate it from large organisations (Fillis, 2002; Gilmore, 2001). SMEs marketing has been characterised by attributes such as haphazard, informal, loose, unstructured, and spontaneous (Gilmore, 2001) compared to "textbook" marketing that seems to have somewhat negative connotations. In addition, SMEs appear to have specific weaknesses with regards to pricing, planning, training, and forecasting (McCartan-Quinn and Carson, 2003). On the other hand, it is argued that a great part of marketing in SMEs is driven by innovation (O'Dwyer, 2009). Moreover, SMEs are seen to operate close to their customers, to be flexible, and to respond quickly to the changing needs of customers (McCartan-Quinn and Carson, 2003). This quick response is part of the SMEs' characteristic that distinguishes them from large organisations.

The special characteristics of SMEs marketing are considered to result from various limitations. According to the literature, marketing functions in SMEs are seen to be hindered by poor cash flow, lack of marketing expertise, business size, tactical and strategic customer-led problems (O'Dwyer, 2009; Simpson and Padmore, 2006; Helen, 2009), narrow customer base, over-reliance on the owner-manager's marketing competency (Stokes 2000), and limited resources relating to finance and time, and limited impact in the marketplace (Gilmore, 2001). With limited resources added to the day-to-day pressures of the business operations, marketing may seem to be peripheral and an unnecessary luxury in SMEs (Hogarth-Scott, 1996).

Special attention is paid to the role of the SMEs owner managers in marketing process as they are seen to be involved in every function of the SMEs. The SMEs owner managers are generalists who have to have a vision of where the business is going and at the same time to take care of the operational details carried out in the firm (Hogarth-Scott, 1996). It is argued that marketing in SMEs is related to the owner-manager's attitudes, experience, and expertise in marketing because these are essentially important than the firm itself (McCartan-Quinn & Carson 2003). The marketing practices adopted in SME are also greatly influenced by the owner-manager's decision-making and inherent skills and abilities (O'Dwyer, 2009). Hogarth-Scott (1996) argued that marketing is often misunderstood and underutilised by SME owner managers and they do not always appear interested to marketing if there is no need for growth or expansion. Furthermore, SMEs owner managers may define marketing as quite narrowly relating only to selling and promoting, but the actual marketing done may still cover a wide range of marketing practices (Stokes, 2000). Stokes (2000) stated that SMEs owner managers spend considerable time and resources on marketing, but they may call it a different manner. The need for marketing is recognised, but often an ad hoc, reactive approach is adopted; for example, the traditional way of looking at marketing with the 4P's is not given much attention (McPherson, 2007). O'Dwyer (2009) stated that there are specific variables and influences according to which marketing is formulated in a way that maximises benefit for an SME. O'Dwyer (2009) further explained that marketing activities in SMEs are shaped through a process where competitors, customers, the business environment, and the limited resources are taken into account.

According to Siu and Kirby (1998), there are four approaches to the role of marketing in small firms. These approaches are as follows: 1) the stages/growth model; 2) the management style model; 3) the management function model; and 4) the contingency model. These approaches are illustrated in Table 2.2. Although each of these approaches contributes to the research of marketing, it still fails to give a comprehensive picture of marketing in SMEs due to lack of empirical evidence of the marketing practices carried out in SMEs.

Sashittal and Jassawalla (2001) found in their study that implementation of marketing in SME consists of day-to-day improvisations and adaptations in marketing strategy and activities. According to them, the nature and extent of marketing improvisations and adaptations determine the level of market orientation, growth, and strategic effectiveness. They argued that marketing planning and implementation interact strongly and this shapes the market behaviours of SMEs and affects the strategic outcomes.

Table 2.2: Four approaches to marketing in small firms

Marketing approach	Description	Critique
Stages/ growth model	Describes the development of a firm through several stages	• low predictive power • limited value as a framework for detailed analysis and planning
Management style approach	Marketing behaviour is related to the motivation, belief, attitude, and objectives of owner-managers	• ignores e.g. organisational structure, owner-manager's marketing decision process and behaviour
Management function approach	Acknowledges marketing as an important function and essential concept for small firm growth, survival and strategic development	• too much or too little emphasis is put on the limitations and constraints of small firms when applying disciplinary foundation of marketing
Contingency approach	Tries to find balance between the limitations of small firms and marketing as a discipline	• variables are not clearly defined, are arbitrarily selected or cannot be measured effectively • is an outcome model, not a process model

Source: Siu and Kirby (1998, p.45)

2.3.2 Market orientation in SMEs

Market orientation does not seem to be related to any specific firm size (Laforet, 2008; Blankson and Cheng 2005). Thus, market orientation is applicable for any types of organisation regardless of the size of the organisation (Blankson, 2006). It is, however, suggested that market orientation gives SMEs a potential competitive advantage over their larger counterparts as they 1) are closer to customers and able to respond immediately, 2) are able to share customer information fast due to less organisational bureaucracy, and 3) can implement marketing plans faster as their marketing plans are rather informal compared to large organisations (Keskin, 2006).

In several literatures, it has been argued that the basis of market orientation - the marketing concept - has not been adopted in a great part of SMEs and one of the reasons for many owner-managers had no formal training in marketing (Peterson, 1989; Meziou, 1991). Peterson (1989) found that many of the SMEs believed that the adoption of marketing concept would result in greater profits but still they were not motivated to do so because profits were not an overriding goal in their business operations.

However, it has been suggested that SMEs may follow some form of self-directed and informal customer-centric philosophies (McPherson, 2007). In empirical findings, it has been shown that SMEs demonstrated customer orientation (Hogarth-Scott, 1996) but this may fall short of what would be considered as a true component of market orientation with reference to Narver and Slater's (1990) definition. For example, according to the responsive market orientation, customer needs are first investigated and assessed, and only then consistent products and services are developed, whereas SMEs owner-managers usually do it contradictory; they develop an offering and then try to find a market for it (Stokes, 2000).

The role of owner managers in adopting market orientation has also been discussed in previous literatures. In this connection, Barnes (2001) suggested that a customer-oriented atmosphere in an SME firm is usually a result of the management style of the owner. He stated that a close contact between the owner and the employees can spread the style to the whole organisation. Moreover, according to Barnes (2001), customer relationship building is in many cases a natural extension of the personalities of the owners and their employees, and this customer relationship building depends on how they communicate with the customers. Coviello (2000) stated that SMEs are more relational than larger firms in some of the marketing processes. SMEs tend to have more interpersonal relationship with their primary customers. SMEs also invest in personal relationships and emphasise on marketing communication that is conducted by the general management itself rather than specialist marketers, and the relationship is directed to a specific customer segment rather than the mass market as whole. Moreover, SMEs place emphasis on direct relationships with specific customers and other players in the market network (Coviello, 2000).

Similarly, owner managers play important roles in developing market-oriented culture in their enterprises (Alpkan *et al.*, 2007) and they are usually crucial in the implementation of market-oriented activities. Owner managers are often the seekers and assimilators of information (Lybaert 1998), although they may not necessarily recognise the need for it (Fuelhart & Glasmeier 2003). Many SMEs are interested in information on their customers and competitors in order for them to be able to differentiate their offerings and positioning, but at the same time, it is only the highly entrepreneurial SMEs that are seen to be active in information acquisition and utilisation (Keh, 2007). Most of the SMEs are regarded as opportunistic in their information seeking behaviours (Fuelhart and Glasmeier 2003) and the main sources of market intelligence appear to be informal (Renko, 2005). Moreover, according to the study by Renko (2005), market intelligence dissemination is not perceived as problematic and is done within an individual enterprise and within a network of firms. At the same time, however, Renko (2005) argued that the interpretation of the information gathered may prove to be challenging in SMEs. On the other hand, the information will be beneficial to SMEs if they use the information accordingly and appropriately (Keh, 2007). In the empirical analysis by Keh (2007), it was found that the use of information for the basis of marketing decisions especially concerning promotion and place has a significant positive influence on SMEs performance.

Vorhies (1999) argued that capabilities are prerequisites of market orientation. In the context of SMEs, it is appropriate to discuss the role of competencies. Hill (2001) defined competencies as underlying characteristics of a person that result in effective and superior performance in a job, and that show themselves as an effective mix of motives, traits, skills, aspects of one's self-image or social role, or as a body of knowledge used by that person. He distinguished competencies that are related to a person from capabilities that integrate the skills, abilities, and learning of several people.

Hill (2001) identified several competencies that are related to effective marketing in SMEs and categorised them into three levels that are linked to each another. Hill (2001) highlighted judgment as a key competency in the decision-making process. He stated that the competency of good judgment is embedded in a combination of other competencies, such as the ability to systematically gather and use market intelligence, the capability to objectively analyse the intelligence as well as the results of one's own actions and decisions, and the ability to learn from experience.

The effect of market orientation on SME performance has been widely investigated (Megicks and Warnaby, 2008). According to Appiah-Adu and Singh (1998), SMEs with a higher degree of customer orientation are likely to be more profitable than their less customer-oriented counterparts. Moreover, innovativeness and proactiveness may positively moderate the relationship between market orientation and SMEs performance (Li, 2008).

2.3.3 Decision-making in Small Medium Enterprises (SMEs)

In SMEs operations, the owner is often one of the top managers and participates in the decision-making process on a daily basis (Miller and Besser, 2005). The owner of the SMEs has a more direct effect on the decision-making process than the CEO of a large corporation (Payne *et al.*, 2005). Generally, the owner of the SMEs has the final word on business decisions and selects the inputs that he or she will accept on each decision (Payne *et al.*, 2005). Since the owner manager has a more direct control of the SMEs business operations, the influences on a single decision-maker appear to be more directly significant to the business (Feltham *et al.*, 2005). In a large operation, the decision process is likely to be more dispersed and institutionalised than in SMEs. This dispersion dilutes the significance of the influences on a single individual to the organisation since the bureaucratic processes are more likely to affect the decisions than does a single manager.

2.3.4   SMEs decision making style

As indicated earlier, the only decision maker in SMEs is the owner-manager. Thus, SMEs owner managers' decision making and management style will have a great deal of impact on how the business is run. In making the decision, the SMEs owner managers confront with a series of restraints, which can narrow their range of choices. These restraints are connected to the limited resources (especially in terms of financial limitation) and those that come from the external environment (in terms of institutions, regulations, market opportunities, geographical location, etc.).

The context of making decision in SMEs is different from the context of making decision in large companies because 1) SMEs owner managers do not have access to solid information like the managers of large companies; 2) SMEs owner managers are confronted with a more hostile external environment (which sometime is considered insignificant for a large company); 3) SMEs owner managers are confronted with repetitive decisions compared to the large companies that often develop routines to manage and make effective use of the managers' time in their managerial activities. On the other hand, decisions made by SMEs owner managers are assumed to be more responsive based on specific issues and situations due to general constraints in terms of material, financial, and human capitals (Varraut, 1999). The simple and functional structure makes the owner manager use his time for current and tactical decisions. The time spent inside the enterprise curtails the owner manager to scan the external environment. Consequently, in the context of a very dynamic and very complex external environment, the rationality of the strategic decisional processes is very weak.

The effect of external environment to the organisational decision making process (including those within SMEs) is significant through different local culture. This refers to as the traditions, the attitudes and certainties, the behavioural rules, and the values that characterise a certain country (Ionescu and Toma, 2001). Some researchers such as Huţu (2003) opined that the local culture has "a greater impact on the employees than the organisational culture, it forms the cultural context for the organisational culture". The most known analysis system of the culture was proposed by Hofstede (1980), which uses four dimensions: uncertainty avoidance, individualism, masculinity, and power distance. In this analysis system, the organisations placed in cultures with high rate on power distance, the centralisation of the decision is remarked. On the other hand, the organisations placed in cultures with low rate on power distance, the decentralisation of the decision is also remarked. But, this can slow down the decision process. Likewise, decision making in collectivist cultures is always made through concession (which sometimes is imposed through pressure), opposing the practice in individualistic cultures where confrontation of ideas is specific and very frequently it arrives to voting for the selection of the best alternative. The influence of local culture in SMEs decision making process can be seen during the starting of decision process, adoption of risk assumption, and the selection criteria for alternative decision. Under these difficult conditions (high uncertainty, insufficient financial, human, information resources, and rapid environment changes), successful SMEs owner managers make decisions on the basis of a skill called "practical intelligence or common sense". The concept was theorised by Sternberg (2004) from Yale University, who defined "practical intelligence or common sense" as "the ability to adapt, shape and select suitable environments".

SMEs decision making and management styles are unique as the owner managers often focus on the short term planning. They are informal in their approach to management practices thus creating decisions based more on personal intuition rather than strategic management tools and they often make very little use of strategic or business planning (Woods and Joyce 2003). Matlay (1999) noted that owner managers made little use of formal decision making tools. In fact, 91.53% of micro-business (less than 10 employees) and 68.05% of small businesses (less than 50 employees) described their management style as informal. Other than that, Woods and Joyce (2003) also concluded that owner managers are more informal in their management style compared to large businesses. Other studies have examined the use of management tools in the decision making and planning processes of SMEs to confirm an informal decision making and management approach. Woods and Joyce (2003) and Stonehouse and Pemberton (2002) found that owner managers made less use of strategic and traditional management tools. Lyles (1996) and Matthews and Scott (1995) determined that small businesses suffered from a lack of sophistication in their approach to strategic management and thinking. Stonehouse and Pemberton (2002) concluded that SMEs rarely engaged in proper planning and often used strategic activities, such as the formation of mission statements, incorrectly or not at all. Furthermore, many SMEs made less use of other traditional decision making procedures (Delisle and St-Pierre 2004). Kotler (2005) and Hisrich (2006) both pointed out that SMEs made little use of marketing information systems, especially market research, when compared to larger enterprises.

According to many literatures concerning SMEs, the owner manager is the central element of the management processes. The management type of the SMEs is considered as being, as a rule, a very centralised one, sometimes concentrated exclusively in the hand of only one person, the owner administrator. Torres (1999) used to this effect the term "egofirm" to define the SME business. Marchesnay (2002) specified that in large companies, the decision-making is substantiated on procedures and interindividual and collective relations. His rationality is that in large companies, there are procedures to follow. In contrast, in SME organisations, the decision-making is done by only one individual, although the individual is surrounded by counsellors.

SME decisions are different from the decisions of managers in large companies, including the assumption of the decision (Gilmore and Carson, 2000). Grieco (2007) stated that managers are associated with routine decisions while SMEs owner managers are associated with non-routine decisions. Busenitz and Barney (1997) stated that SMEs owner managers are more inclined towards experimental manner in making decision than the managers of large companies. It can also be suggested that SMEs owner managers are people specialising in making decision intuitively despite the rare resources (Casson, 1991).

The SMEs are assumed to have specific characteristics that are distinct from those of the non-entrepreneurs, which may influence the decisional process (Mador, 2000). One of the main characteristics is the way of perceiving the risks; they have the tendency to generalise the experiences very easily and to believe that they will succeed.

The decision-making style also differs among different categories of owner manager (Gustafsson, 2006). The beginner tends to adopt a more analytical and systematic style of processing information (Ucbasaran, 2008) and, implicitly, assumes a more rigorously validated decision. Typical owner managers, who have a very large experience, appeal more frequently to experimental refinement of information. When conditions imply a decision in a complex, unknown situation, the decision-makers try to structure the initial data in proportion to previous experiences or knowledge. Therefore, the new circumstances are adjusted to the old decisional situations and the same techniques used previously are applied. Such an approach, although faster, can be rather risky under the conditions of the contemporary business environment when the characteristics of the market change rapidly and require a management of change. The tendency of over-generalisation starting from a few elements of the decisional situation (Busenitz and Barney, 1997) can lead to a loss of ability of being proactive.

There are also important differences between the first generation of entrepreneurs and the following ones. Alderson (2009) showed that the decision making in first generation firms is more centralised than the following one, which is likely to adapt more professional management style. Moreover, Alderson (2009) showed that although they sensibly differ from the first generation, the next generations of owner managers (especially about the family enterprises) orientate after the value of the enterprise (ruled by the founder), which they use as a decisional instrument, when they confront with a difficult decision in which they have very few information.

It has also been found that SMEs lack knowledge and practice of benchmarking the performance measures when making decisions. Cassel (2001) found that there is a lack of benchmarking in SMEs coupled with an actual lack of interest in the subject matter. Cassel's findings supported earlier work completed by Monkhouse (1995), who concluded that SMEs do not engage in benchmarking in any significant fashion. Hudson, Lean and Smart (2001) agreed with Cassel's findings with one exception – that financial benchmarking is common in SMEs. However, financial benchmarking was categorised as ineffective in supporting the goals of the organisation. Other studies have found that SMEs rarely used performance measures, and when they do, they are often used the performance measures incorrectly (Veitch and Smith, 2000; Husdon, 2000). Additionally, McMahon and Holmes (1991) determined that the majority of SMEs made little use of formal techniques that were common in large businesses. The researchers determined that there was very little financial analysis being conducted and that only 20%

to 30% of SMEs were involved in budgeting. Peel and Bridge (1998) looked specifically at the use of capital budgeting in SME planning and decision making, and concluded that the majority of firms made use of less sophisticated financial tools. Similar results by Lazaridis (2004) found that 11.39% of SMEs made use of recommended financial analysis techniques.

2.3.5   SMEs marketing decision characteristics

The extant literatures used numerous terms to describe the phenomenon of SMEs marketing decision making or concept closely related to it. Gilmore *et al.* (2001) described SMEs marketing decisions as a matter of routine; the SME manager perhaps does not even realise that he is making them. The decision making is likely to be haphazard and apparently informal, according to personal and business priorities at any given point in time (Gilmore *et al.*, 2001). This supported Simon's (1960) definition that SME decision making is a continuum ranging from routine programmed decisions to unpredictable, non-programmed or intuitive decisions. SMEs marketing decision making is haphazard and informal because of inadequate understandings on how small businesses can make their strategic marketing decisions (Culkin and Smith, 2000). Despite significant interventions by the Government and professional advisors to change the paradigm, the way SMEs make their marketing decision is still bounded by the nature of their business. Hill (2001) in his study suggested that the decision-making in respect of marketing activities in SMEs is distinctly characterised by the use of networks. This concurs with Webster (1992) and Hill and McGowan (1996) who stated that contact networks actually enhance and add quality to marketing decisions in SMEs. Networking is defined as a naturally inherent aspect of SMEs owner manager decision making, particularly those decisions relating to marketing. This is because SMEs must go outside the businesses physical confines in order to do business and this business is a marketing-led activity. Thus, SMEs are doing marketing through their natural and inherent networking activity, through all their normal communication activities, such as interacting and participating in social, business, and trade activities. Some of the characteristics of "marketing by networking" are that it is based around people-orientated activities, it is informal, often discreet, interactive, interchangeable, integrated, habitual, and can either be passive or proactive.

Abdullah (2002) found in their study that 40% of SMEs occasionally collected and processed marketing information, and 20% have formal procedures to disseminate this information within the firm. Since market research is crucial in making decisions and planning strategy, in its absence many owner managers are left to use intuition or feedback from family and friends in making crucial decisions (Hisrich, 2006).

2.3.6 SMEs marketing decision making process

The literatures on SME marketing decision making mainly focus on behavioural intentions e.g. effective SMEs marketing (Hills, 2001), SMEs marketing in practice (Gilmore *et al.*, 2001), and marketing in SMEs (Simpson *et al.*, 2006). Only a few researchers have attempted to explain the process of the events leading to decision making behaviour (Nichola, 2004). Research into SMEs marketing decision making remains inadequate in understanding how small businesses currently make their marketing decisions.

The most widely accepted model of decision making process was proposed by Mintzberg (1976), who suggested seven steps in decision-making, namely: recognition of the problem, diagnosis of the problem, searching the necessary information, design of possible alternatives, the alternatives screening, evaluation/choice, the authorisation (including persons responsible for implementing the decision). These steps are illustrated in Figure 2.4. This model has been challenged by Hansson (2005) who argued that human beings cannot gather information without in some way simultaneously developing alternatives, and in doing this they are forced to a decision. In this model, the objective of decision maker is to choose the best alternative and to make the correct decision. However, when the information needed is not available, it is not possible to optimise the decision under uncertainty. Furthermore, when a decision is required before the needed information can be obtained, this approach is left lacking. Although this approach is the ideal model under ideal circumstances, there is a need to make decisions in less-than-ideal circumstances.

Figure 2.4: A general model of the strategic decision process

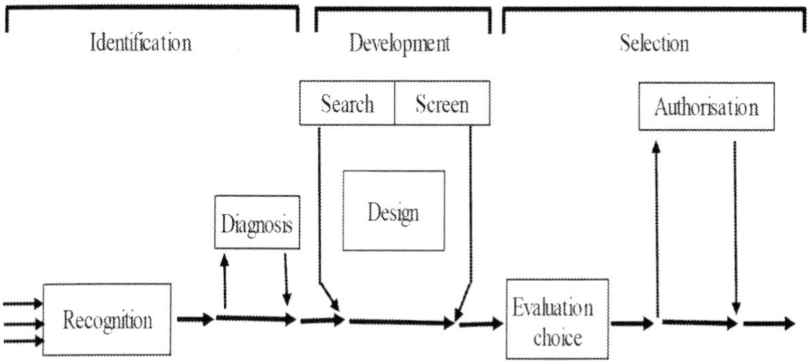

Source: Adopted from Radu (2010, p.5)

In response to model proposed by Mintzberg (1976), Gibcus and van Hoesel (2004) proposed three stages and two moments in decision making process to understand many of the mechanisms of the decisional process that is specific for the SMEs as shown in Figure 2.5. The callout of the model helps to understand many of the mechanisms of the decisional process that is specific for SMEs.

The first stage is a process of generating the idea or nurture stage. In this stage, most of the decision makers do not think about alternative solutions. The first idea, sometimes with minor adjustments, develops into a decision. This is an indication of the predominance of emotional elements. Even if there is no pressure in the decision making, the decision makers do not develop alternative solutions.

Before going to the next stage, a mediate step is needed – trigger and informal decision. The trigger is a motivation that induces the decision maker to refine the idea. Depending on the intensity of the idea and the incubation period, the releaser must be more powerful or weaker, direct or indirect. The informal decision is not written; it manifests as an intention in the decision maker's mind, a verbal agreement between the associates.

After making the informal decision, next is the elaboration of the idea. In this stage, the alternative idea remains unaffected. The idea mainly acts as a feeler to the basic idea to analyse the costs and benefits. Consulting with third parties such bankers, advisors, and employees is also crucial at this stage. The risks and potential obstacles are also identified (most of the times this activity is superficial; when a relatively correct dimensioning is done, there could be interference from an over-appreciation of the personal capacities from the enterprise itself to overtop these problems). After this stage, another crucial moment intervenes in the decision-making process i.e., the formal decision.

The third stage assumes the implementation of the decision. The main problems that the SME owner confronts in this stage are financial problems where the difficulties they encounter do not discourage the entrepreneurs and do not encourage them to revise their decision. There are various weaknesses identified in this model such as the elements connected to the personal competency, the influences by the family, and the ignorance of the SME's experience. This model also does not highlight the influence of some constraints connected to the financial resources very clearly.

Figure 2.5: A model of the decision-making process by SMEs

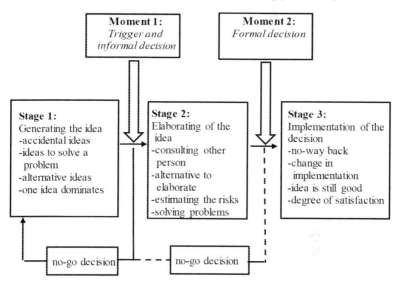

Source: Gibcus and van Hoesel (2004)

Jocumsen (2002) in his study proposed distinct steps in the strategic marketing decision-making process in SMEs. The core of the model is a series of three loosely defined steps or tasks (information gathering/research, financial analysis and assessment, and internal matter), which are conducted non-sequentially but preceded by a "decision initiation" and followed by "final commitment". These steps are illustrated in Figure 2.6

The model suggests that SMEs owner managers make extensive use of learned competencies (in the forms of "perceived" rationality), basic analytical tools, and considerable written activity. Furthermore, they make equally extensive use of inherent competencies, mostly in the form of intuition and gut feel, which are acknowledged by respondents as arising from both innate sources and learning experiences. Finally, use of internal networks is restricted almost exclusively to family and use of external networks is minimal and restricted to bankers, accountants, and Government departments.

However, the influence of internal factors such as decision importance, firm size, success of business, organisational structure, education level of manager, and risk is not discussed in the model.

Figure 2.6: SMEs strategic marketing decision making process

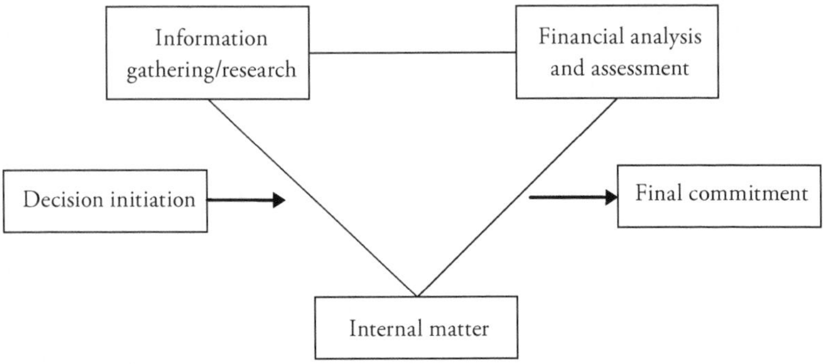

Where:

- **Information gathering/research** includes, for example, marketing related research, general information, technical issues and information about the general environment.
- **Financial analysis and assessment** includes financial analysis, budgeting, spreadsheet analysis, and examining alternative options
- **Internal matters** includes long term business view, goal setting, family, personal and lifestyle consideration, and ethical and social consideration.

Source: Jocumsen (2002)

The managerial decision-making process as illustrated in Figure 2.7 was proposed by Harrison and Pelletier (2000). This model consists of six areas that are all interrelated and form a dynamic process. The decision making process starts with setting the managerial objectives. These managerial objectives are within definitive time and cost constraints and usually originate from an external need or opportunity (Harrison and Pelletier, 2000). Later, the manager usually starts to search for alternatives, compares and evaluates the different alternatives, and then creates an action plan for implementing it. The evaluation and comparison of the different alternatives are greatly influenced by the personal characteristics of the person or the team that is in control. A clear characteristic that affects the final decision is given by Harrison and Pelletier (2000) who explained that the risk acceptance is often the most important decisive factor. After the decision is made and a plan of action has been formed, the decision should be actually implemented, and then followed up and controlled. Since the managerial decision making process is dynamic, it is also possible to go back several times. This means that after analysing the results of a step, the decision maker can go back and try to get to a better input for that particular part of the process.

Figure 2.7: The managerial decision making process

Setting managerial objectives	Revise Objectives	Searching for alternatives		Comparing and evaluating alternatives

Take corrective action

Renew search

Follow up and control		Implement decisions		The act of choice

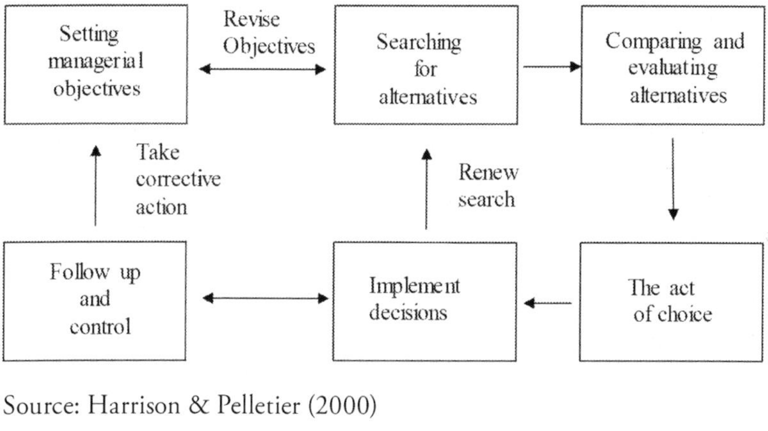

Source: Harrison & Pelletier (2000)

From the four models presented, it is a question as to what extent the SMEs owner managers are rational in the decision making processes they develop. Radu (2009) considered that the SMEs owner managers do not have time to go through a thorough, rational decision-making process. He suggested that, under the conditions of an environment with a high degree of uncertainty, the SMEs owner managers act inspirationally, neglecting any procedure or rule that has been used previously. Hence, it can be said here that the decision process in SME is very much inspired by the personal characteristics of the SMEs owner managers, which are missing or are not clearly presented in these models. The influence of SMEs owner managers in the performance of decision process has been extensively discussed by Mador (2000) and Radu (2009).

2.4   Research Framework – A model of SME marketing decision making process in Malaysia

From the previous discussion, it is clear that decision makers can use a number of different decision making models and styles, and none of these models is generally accepted for SME environment (Joensuu, 2009; Reijonen, 2010; Tamara, 2010, Sarah, 2012). Within the traditional framework of decision making, there is a basic distinction between what the decision makers want and what they believe is true (Hastie, 2001; Kieren, 2007). The rational expectations principle proposes that each decision alternative is considered by evaluating its expected satisfaction (or dissatisfaction) with the probability of the consequences occurring. However, this theory neither accounts for information sources nor account for how these sources are weighted in the decision making process. While the theory is limited and does not provide a full description of decision making, it is still the dominant conceptual framework for studies into rational decision making (Hastie 2001; Kieren, 2007).

In real life, decision can be influenced by three categories of factors, which are environmental factors, organisational factors, and specific factors for the decision that add values to the decision maker. These factors may be real, hypothetical, qualitative, or quantitative (Kieren, 2007; Ogarca, 2010). The influences of these factors are different from one decision maker to another decision maker, and it is influenced by the number of factors, both internal and external. It is of great importance to SME decision makers to find out what factor significantly influences other decision maker. This is to improve the SME decision maker's approach in the decision process in order not to repeat the same mistake as the others have done (Anna & Peter, 2007). In this study, there is a difference in the influence of driving factor from the internal and external perspectives. The difference is that the external factors are seldom affected by managers' decision, are external to SME organisation, and may be regarded as a parameter of the marketing decision process. This is because external factors are unlikely to have decisive influence on the decision process in general (Anna & Peter, 2007), and can only encourage or discourage a decision maker in the decision process. On the other hand, internal factors are internal aspects over which the decision maker has a control. These factors include all resources and activities that facilitate the decision maker to perform the marketing decision process. It can be concluded here that the external factors consist of determinants regarding environment factor, while the internal factors are determined by the specific factors. In order to develop such a model for the theoretical framework in this research, a refinement of the basic decision making model (see Figure 2.1) is required. This refined model is depicted in Figure 2.8 and encompasses internal and external aspects of decision factors.

However, the model depicted in Figure 2.8 has limitations. In SME environment, structured decision making processes are rarely used, and most decisions are reached in an unstructured, hermeneutic fashion (Khalifa et al., 2001; Lin & Pervan, 2001; Kieren, 2007). Decisions often do not cohere, are not logical, and depend systematically on factors such as context, mood, and the method of data presentation (Shafir & LeBoeuf, 2002). More importantly, the influences of decision are often overlooked (Kieren, 2007: Lynch, 2011 & Metts, 2011, Richard, 2013). Decision makers in real life play a significant role in the decision process particularly the impact of personal competency to outcome of the decision.

They usually directly and/or indirectly dominate decision making in their organisations. In previous discussion about decision making model, the role of decision maker has been lightly highlighted or not highlighted at all. Lau (2011) and Richard (2013) point out that the success of SMEs very much depends on decision makers' characteristics. Furthermore, there is also an increasing likelihood that decision makers' characteristics will affect the way in which information is framed and evaluated. This leads to the conclusion that no matter how the decision elements are interacted to reach the decision, decision makers play an important role in shaping the decision outcome (Kieren, 2007).

Figure 2.8: Refined Decision Making Model

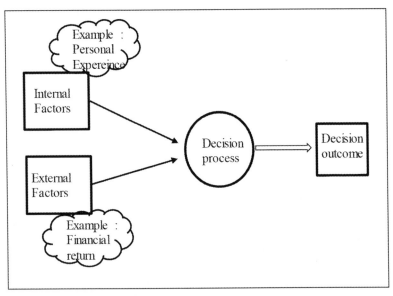

As discussed previously, the rationality of decision processes reduces as the complexity increases (Maritan, 2001; Kieren, 2009). Furthermore, there is also an increasing likelihood that driving factors will affect the way in which information is framed and evaluated. Many factors that affect decision making in marketing process can be readily identified. However, it is uncertain what direct effects these factors have on decisions outcomes. From the literature, it appears that factors can be categorised as sources of information and driving factors that act on the decision process, rational or not, to produce decision outcomes. In this study, the proposed marketing decision model was based on basic decision making model by the work of Einhorn & Hogarth (1981), as depicted in Figure 2.1. The model forms the basis for this study. From the model, it can be seen that a number of internal and external factors affect a decision outcome and the decision making process. The key element of this model is the explicit acknowledgement of the effects of decision makers' characteristics over both the decision making process and the information that is used to produce decision outcomes. Information in this study refers to "a body of facts in a format that facilitates decision making defines relationships between pieces of data" (Zikmund, 2003; Kieren, 2007). The data are processed in such a way that they increase the knowledge of the person using it. In this model, decision makers provide the lens or environment in which information is examined, and shape both the way the decision is made and the way in which the information is used. Figure 2.9 depicts a refinement of the decision making model that accounts for the role of decision maker factor.

An important element of the revised model is that the process, or how the decision is made, becomes a function of the organisational and decision context. As previously discussed, structured decision making processes are rare. Furthermore, this model supports the findings by Kieren (2007) that the decision process depends on a number of different factors interacting in the process. In this model, the decision process is treated as a black box where only the inputs and outputs should be examined. There is no longer a need to distinguish between rationale or behaviour decision processes. The final component of the model is that it acknowledges that decision outcomes can be either measurable or nonquantifiable.

Figure 2.9: Proposed SME Marketing Decision Making Process Model

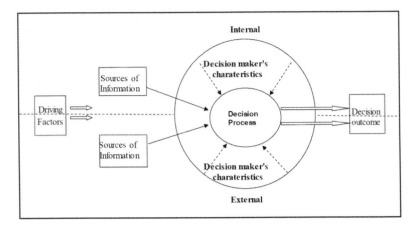

2.4.1 Factor interaction

The interplay between information and the driving factor in which it is processed can mean that it is sometimes difficult to determine if a driving factor is under active consideration as a piece of information, or is acting as an influence. In some instances, driving factor may also be represented by a piece of information. For example, the personal experience of the decision makers may mean that a decision is taken based of informational assessment of the similar or close instance. A driving factor may also provide the necessary environment for information to be considered. For example, a decision maker may concern about ethical and social consideration in business, as this may be part of his corporate social responsibility. This factor creates an organisational awareness of such issues, thus these issue are considered in the decision making process. However, in other organisations, without this concern, this information might not be considered.

Moreover, in this model, driving factor is categorised as internal or external. The internal factor includes past experiences (Rocha, de Mello, Pacheco, de Abreu Farias, 2012; Nielsen & Nielsen, 2010;

Gray & McNaughton, 2010; Richard E. Game, 2013), goal setting (Robert, 2002), personal competency (Hill *et al.*, 2001), firm size (Ji & Junzhe, 2010), and financial capability (Tamara, 2010). Risk has also been traditionally treated as an internal factor as it deals with decision maker perception. However, it is argued that risk is often difficult to control (Karla Díaz, Ute Rietdorf & Utz Dornberger, 2011). In many instances, risk is categorised as an external factor. Factors that attract uncertainty must be treated as external. Often these factors have been overlooked in traditional decision making models. For example, it is difficult to justify marketing decision because of long-term business relationship as compared to estimated quantifiable financial return (Uma & Bhuvanes, 2011). From the literature, many decisions have made based on hunches, impressions, biases, and unquantifiable perceptions. However, because these factors do not appear in traditional decision making models, they also never appear as decision justifications. Other external factors include financial return (Uma & Bhuvanes, 2011) and long-term business relationship (Kieren, 2007; O'Dwyer, 2010). In many of the decision models, this classification has been one of convenience as most models are unable to account for internal or external factors. While internal factors are the most predominant factor in decision justifications, it would seem that in some factors play only a limited role in the decision making process.

Information is evaluated within a given context or environment. Some of these information factors have already been recognized as affecting decision making processes (Sarkis & Sundarraj, 2000; Keh *et al.*, 2007; Cacciolatti *et al.*, 2011; Krishan *et al.*, 2012). Examples of these include past experience (Stephane, 2010; Nielsen & Nielsen, 2011; Musso, Barbara & Francioni, 2012) and family (Manuel, 2013). This information will be evaluated by the decision maker to weighting the importance of individual information factors.

2.4.2 Decision factors

Factors that affect decision making are grouped into three categories: source of information, driving factor and decision maker. This section examines the types of information used to make decisions and the characteristic of the decision maker that act as influences. Finally, the relationship of factor and decision outcomes is discussed.

2.4.2.1 Information

The effective use of information can produce a number of benefits for SMEs, including lesser uncertainty, more effective alternatives, and more effective decision. Information can be defined as signs of reference that may take the form of knowledge, wisdom, or raw data (Riley 2003) that form a "body of facts that are in a format suitable for decision making" (Zikmund, 2003). Information can be categorised into one or more groups including tangible, intangible, financial, quantitative, and qualitative (Sarkis & Sundarraj, 2000). In this study, information can be divided into internal and external information as defined by Sarkis and Sundarraj (2000). Examples of internal information include past experience (Musso & Francioni, 2012) and formal education (Musso & Francioni, 2012). External information includes customer (Elaine *et al.*, 2007), other business managers (Elaine *et al.*, 2007), SMEs associations (Syahira, 2009), and government agencies such as SME Corp. and Matrade (Elaine, 2007; Richard, 2007). It is the opinion of some authors (e.g., Buss (1987); Mintzberg, (1972) that external information is more important than internal information when it comes to making a decision.

2.4.2.2 Decision makers' characteristics

The main part of the proposed model is the demographics of SMEs owner managers, including age, gender, ethnicity, and education level (Leepaibon, 2007). The reason for this is simple. While owner (shareholder) of large company employs professional managers, most SMEs owner managers prefer to manage their firm themselves. Therefore, it would seem reasonable to expect that the abilities, behavioural patterns, and demographic profile of SMEs owner managers would have great impact on their decision compared to the managers in large companies. Elaine (2007) highlights the influence of decision makers' characteristics as the major source of business information for SMEs. Therefore, issues relating to the owner managers' age, gender, ethnicity, and education level will be discussed in the following subsection.

- **Age of owner managers**

Entrepreneurs vary in age, from young to old. In many instances, an individual may begin a business as a hobby or secondary source of income, and then it grows into a profit-driven enterprise. A number of studies have examined the effect of the owners' age on the business (e.g., Rocha, de Mello, Pacheco, de Abreu Farias, 2012; Nielsen & Nielsen, 2010; Gray & McNaughton, 2010). Heck, Rowe, and Owen (1995) conclude that the typical owners are older and more educated than younger entrepreneurs. It is thought that the hassles of commuting and the trend of corporate downsizing as well as the lifestyle changes of many would explain the increased age of the typical owners. Older business owners are more likely to continue to operate a business instead of returning to be an employee of another company. According to Gray and McNaughton (2010), many of the current owners of business have been in the fields for a number of years, and have brought with them years of experiences. Therefore, it is likely that the age of the owners could affect the way they make the decision.

- **Gender**

The gender of business owners, while it may seem somewhat discriminatory or biased, may in fact have a significant impact on the performance of the company. Several studies have identified gender difference in terms of decision process and performance (e.g., Spiling & Berg, 2000; Coleman 2000; Ho, 2011; Mahmood & Hanafi, 2012). It is interesting to investigate this issue in making marketing decision.

- **Ethnicity**

The Malaysian business scenario is unique in the sense of the multiple ethnic groups operating and behaving in unique ways, the ways perceived the best to them (Mohd Sobri, 2010). Insights show that certain ethnic groups dominate certain types of business. According to Salimah *et al.* (2007) and Shukor (2006), most of the SMEs in Malaysia are owned by the Malaysian Chinese community. The Chinese are said to have been dominating the business in Malaysia for a long time. For example, Gomez (2004) reports that the Chinese people have owned 50% of equity of the construction sector, 82% of wholesales trade, 58% of retail trade, and about 40% of the manufacturing factor.

The Malay ethnic group that dominates the political and administrative environment since the establishment of Malaysia is yet to perform diligently in business. There are reports and claims the Malaysian Government has given priority to the indigenous people, in particular the Malay, in offering supports and assistances to ensure the economic stability among the ethnic groups.

Other ethnic groups also play their part in the country's economic development. For example, the Malaysian Indians have been said to be dominant in certain service industries such as money exchange business, cleaning, and hair cutting. The key issue highlighted here is that it seems all the ethnicities operate within each group's contact and domain, which could influence the way they approach the decision process (Donald, 2010).

- **Education Level**

In the past, many entrepreneurs left school at an early age to pursue their business interests (Knowles & White, 1995). Business owners are a diverse group as they vary in terms of education level. Wasilczuk (2000) examined the relationship between education of the owner managers and the growth of the business. She concludes that persons with higher education managed firms with higher growth perspective, while persons with lower education managed those with lower growth perspective. She also noted that those decision makers with higher education were more often than others to read professional literature, to attend more courses, and to seek the advice of consultants. They were more interested in their personal growth and development as individuals. As business owners with more education are more likely to manage business with greater growth potential, it is possible that they are more structured in the process of making decision (Elaine, 2007; Fabio, 2012; Richard, 2013).

2.4.2.3 Driving factors

As discussed previously, there are many driving factors that affect the way in which an organisation approaches the decision making process. These factors do not necessarily have a direct influence on the outcomes of decisions, but may instead act on the information that is being fed into the process. For example, the influence of profit margin will determine which pieces of information are acknowledged in an evaluation or justification process (Brindle. 1999; O'Reilly, 1990; Kieren, 2007; Uma & Bhuvanes, 2011). It is a combination of driving factors, information, and the decision process that lead to decision outcomes. The lack of understanding in marketing decision making highlights a gap in the literature, thus further investigation is required. The actual decision factors, how they interact, and what effects they have on outcomes are unknown. In order to investigate this problem, a great understanding of why the factors are not disclosed needs to be achieved. This research will examine this issue.

2.4.3 Relationships between driving factors and decision outcomes

Several driving factors that influence decision making have been discussed in previous section. Understanding the factors influencing decision making process is important to understand what decisions are made. That is, the factors that influence the process may impact the outcomes. After a decision is made, decision maker may experience various reactions. Several of the outcomes that may result from a decision are satisfaction or dissatisfaction, both of which may influence a future decision. Some case studies have noted that driving factors are not explicitly acknowledged in decision outcome (see for examples Davis *et al.* (1992), Myers (1994a; 1994b), Ramiller (2001), and Heracleous and Barrett (2001). Hence, it is interesting to understand the relationship between driving factor and decision outcome in the context of this study.

2.5   Hypotheses

The hypotheses on the proposed framework are based on the findings from previous studies. The hypotheses are linked to decision makers' characteristics, sources of information, driving factors, and decision making method.

2.5.1   Hypotheses linked to driving factors

Many studies have acknowledged the effect of driving factors in the process of making decision (Jocumsen, 2002; Elaine, 2007; Joensuu, 2009). These factors do not necessarily have a direct influence on the outcomes of decisions, but may instead act on the information fed into the process (Kieren, 2007). We propose the following hypothesis to answer the effect of driving factor on the adoption of decision method.

Ho1   *There is a relationship between the driving factor and the decision outcome.*

2.5.2   Hypotheses linked to source of information

Most studies have concluded that the marketing decision making process in SMEs environment is informal and haphazard (Gilmore *et al.*, 2001) due to its heavy reliance on personal networking. However, some researchers have argued that the appropriate source of information can play a role in determining the method adopted in the process (Jocumsen, 2002). Elaine (2007) highlights the influence of decision makers' characteristics as the major sources of business information for SMEs. The following are hypotheses to answer the influence of decision makers' characteristics on the adoption source of information.

Ho2   *There is a significant difference among the genders of SMEs decision makers in adoption of source of information.*

Ho3   *There is a significant difference among the ages of SMEs decision makers in adoption of source of information.*

Ho4   *There is a significant difference among the ethnicities of SMEs decision makers in the adoption of source of information.*

Ho5   *There is a significant difference among the education levels of SMEs decision makers in the adoption of source of information.*

2.5.3   Hypotheses linked to decision making method

It is interesting to examine the effect of decision makers' characteristics to the adoption of decision method. The following hypotheses are developed to answer the relationship.

Ho6   *There is a significant difference among the genders of SMEs decision makers in adoption of decision method.*

Ho7   *There is a significant difference among the ages of SMEs decision makers in adoption of decision method.*

Ho8   *There is a significant difference among the ethnicities of SMEs decision makers in the adoption of decision method.*

Ho9   *There is a significant difference among the education levels of SMEs decision makers in the adoption of decision method.*

2.5.4   Hypotheses linked to decision outcome

Previous studies have shown a positive correlation between the effective decision making process and the decision outcome (Kieren, 2007). Hence, it is interesting to understand the effect of different decision methods on the decision outcome. The following hypothesis is developed to answer the relationship.

Ho10   *There is a relationship between the decision method used in the decision making process and the decision outcome.*

2.6   Summary

In brief, this chapter has reviewed the relevant literatures with the present study. This chapter also has identified the gaps in the existing body of knowledge, and eventually developed the research theoretical model incorporated in two main parts. In the first part, the extant theories of organisation decision making have been reviewed. In the second part, the extant literatures of SMEs marketing decision making process have been discussed to form a basis for development of research framework. This chapter also presents research framework used in this study.

CHAPTER 3

RESEARCH METHDOLOGY

3.0   Introduction

The main objective of this chapter is to discuss the research design and the construction of qualitative research (interview) and quantitative research (questionnaire survey) to investigate the process of marketing decision making for Small Medium Enterprises (SMEs) in Malaysia. The discussion includes selection of scales for measurement, sampling, sample size, pre-test and pilot tests, recruitment of participants, data collection techniques, and data analysis techniques. Finally, measurement of validity and reliability is discussed.

3.1   Research Design

The research method used in this study involved both qualitative and quantitative components, as this research investigated the behaviour of SME decision makers. The use of mixed methods, combining both qualitative and quantitative components in this research design, is in accordance with a growing trend in the social and behavioural sciences (Tashakkori & Teddlie, 1998; Patton 2002; Creswell *et al.*, 2006; Karen, 2007; Chen, 2012). As suggested by Tashakkori and Teddlie (1998), research questions in studies of social and behavioural sciences are best answered with mixed methods rather than using only either qualitative or quantitative method.

Patton (2002) further emphasises that it is common that quantitative and qualitative methods are used in a complementary fashion to answer different questions that do not easily come together to provide a single, well-integrated picture of the situation. Sekaran (2000) points out that the use of a combination of methods is likely to reduce the biases and to increase the validity and reliability of the research data. Consequently, mixed methods were used in this study for both data collection and analysis.

Mixed methods research by definition is "the type of research in which a researcher or team of researchers combines elements of qualitative and quantitative research approaches (e.g., use of qualitative and quantitative viewpoints, data collection, analysis, inference techniques) for the broad purposes of breadth and depth of understanding and corroboration" (Johnson et al., 2007, p.123). This research methodology is argued to be intellectual and practical, as it is likely to take the advantage of overcoming the weaknesses in singular methods (Johnson & Onwuegbuzie, 2004), and to provide the most informative, complete, balanced, and useful research results (Johnson et al., 2007; Chen, 2012). The use of mixed methods as distinct from either qualitative or quantitative methodology is growing in popularity, and this approach has been more widely recognised with the publication of a number of studies dealing specifically with mixed methodologies (e.g., Chen, 2012; Karen, 2007; Creswell, 2006; Tashakkori & Teddle, 2003). These studies represent significant advancement in the recognition of mixed methods as an alternative to qualitative or quantitative approach. Importantly, these researchers have also sought to provide a framework that explains and recognises the different approaches taken within the mixed methods frame, rather than classifying them all broadly as mixed methodologies.

Based upon the overall purpose of the study and the research questions identified, the research used a mixed method approach to investigate issue relating to SME marketing decision making. The conceptual framework used to guide the study was developed as a result of the literature review, as shown in Figure 2.8. In this study, a mixed method approach was adopted to allow for initial generation of rich data in relation to the relatively unexplored area of SME marketing decision making process, and then to expand this knowledge with added benefits of a broader study to reveal more general findings. Rocco *et al.* (2003) and Karen (2007) suggest that studies utilising mixed method for this reason are "explicitly seeking a synergistic benefit from integrating both the post-positivist and constructivist paradigms". The underlying assumption is that research is stronger when it mixes research paradigms, because a fuller understanding of human phenomenon is gained" (Rocco *et al.*, 2003, p.21). This research aimed to exploit the strengths of both the qualitative and quantitative approaches to research, and obtain the synergy described by Rocco *et al.* (2003).

This particular research was categorised as development as it proposed to utilise the outcomes from one method to develop and inform the other. The initial qualitative data collection method, referred to as Phase One, was used to inform a second stage of quantitative data collection, Phase Two. This approach can be categorised as a two-phase approach (Creswell, 2006), with the advantage of this particular mixed method approach being that the two paradigms are clearly separate, thus enable a researcher to present thoroughly the paradigm assumptions behind each phase. Therefore, throughout the description and explanation of the methodology for this study in this chapter, the two phases will be described separately to ensure the differing perspectives are adequately represented.

The approach taken in this research was a sequential exploratory design or two-phase approach, as shown in Figure 3.1a. Creswell *et al.* (2003) suggest that the intent of the two-phase exploratory design is that the results of the first method (qualitative) can help develop or inform the second method (quantitative). This design is based on the premise that an exploration is needed for one of several reasons: Measures or instruments are not available, the variables are unknown, or there is no guiding framework or theory. Because this design begins qualitatively, it is best suited for exploring a phenomenon (Creswell *et al.*, 2003). This design is particularly useful when a researcher needs to develop and test an instrument because the instrument is still not available (Creswell *et al.*, 2006), or identify important variables to study quantitatively when the variables are unknown. It is also appropriate when a researcher wants to generalise the results to different groups (Morse, 1991), to test aspects of an emergent theory or classification (Morgan, 1998), or to explore a phenomenon in depth and then measure its prevalence.

In exploratory design procedures, the process starts with qualitative data to explore a phenomenon, and then builds to a second, quantitative phase (see Figure 3.1a). Researchers using this design build on the results of the qualitative phase by developing an instrument, identifying variables, or stating propositions for testing based on an emergent theory or framework. These developments connect the initial qualitative phase to the subsequent quantitative component of the study. Because the design begins qualitatively, a greater emphasis is often placed on the qualitative data. Myers and Oetzel's (2003) study on organisational assimilation is an example of an exploratory design. They first explore the topic qualitatively and develop themes from their qualitative data. They then develop an instrument based on these results and subsequently use this instrument in the second, quantitative phase of the study.

Figure 3.1: The Exploratory Design

(a) Exploratory Design

(b) Exploratory Design: Instrument Development Model

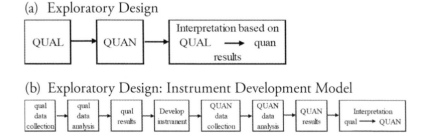

(c) Exploratory Design: Taxonomy Development Model

Source: Sequential Exploratory Design (Creswell, 2006, p.19)

This design has two common variants, the instrument development model and the taxonomy development model. Each of these models begins with an initial qualitative phase, and ends with a quantitative phase. They differ in the way the researcher connects the two phases (see Figure 3.1b and 3.1c) and in the relative emphasis of the two methods.

Researchers use the instrument development model (see Figure 3.1b) to develop and implement a quantitative instrument based on qualitative findings. In this design, the researcher first qualitatively explores the research topic with a few participants. The qualitative findings then guide the development of items and scales for a quantitative survey instrument.

In the second data collection phase, the researcher implements and validates this instrument quantitatively. In this design, the qualitative and quantitative methods are connected through the development of the instrument items. Researchers using this variant often emphasise the quantitative aspect of the study. For the current research, using this model, initially the researcher qualitatively explored the experience of SME decision makers about the making of marketing decision in their organisation (that is, how they perceive the process in the making decision). Based on their qualitative results, the researcher developed an instrument, and then implemented it in the second quantitative phase.

The taxonomy development model (see Figure 3.1c) occurs when the initial qualitative phase is conducted to identify important variables, to develop a taxonomy or classification system, or to develop an emergent theory, and the secondary, quantitative phase tests or studies these results in more detail (Morgan, 1998;

Tashakkori & Teddlie, 1998). In this model, the initial qualitative phase produces specific categories or relationships. These categories or relationships are then used to direct the research questions and data collection used in the second, quantitative phase. This model is used when a researcher formulates quantitative research questions or hypotheses based on qualitative findings, and proceeds to conduct a quantitative study to answer the questions. In addition, a researcher may identify emergent categories from the qualitative data, and then use the quantitative phase to examine the prevalence of these categories within different samples (Morse, 1991), or use taxonomy affiliation as a basis for identifying comparison groups. For example, Goldenberg, Gallimore, and Reese (2005) describe how they identified new variables and hypotheses about predictors of family literacy practices based on their qualitative case study. They then conducted a quantitative path analysis study to test these qualitatively identified variables and relationships.

In this present research, it was split into two distant phases namely a qualitative phase (Phase One) and a quantitative phase (Phase Two). Detailed explanation of each research phases including overview, sampling method, data collection, and data analysis methods are discussed in this chapter. The issues of reliability and validity of each phase and the ethical considerations of the project are also discussed. Results of Phase One are presented in Chapter Four, and results of Phase Two are presented in Chapter Five. The process flow of the research is shown in Figure 3.2

3.2   Phase One: Qualitative Phase

Phase One was the qualitative phase of the project, and was aimed at exploring the experience of SME decision maker in making a marketing decision. Based on the conceptual framework developed from the literature review, a research process appropriate to addressing the research questions was identified for use during this phase. This phase consisted of the collection of interview data from individuals identified as decision makers in the organisation in which they worked. The data were analysed against the conceptual framework to identify converging or diverging areas of interest. Finally, a cross-case analysis was conducted to draw together the findings in preparation for Phase Two.

The interview process was conducted with SMEs decision makers from different organisations. They were Organisation A, Organisation B, organisation C, and Organisation D. Findings from these data were not only employed in the quantitative questionnaire design for larger survey, but were also used later for comparison with results from the quantitative survey. This section includes five main areas for discussion as follows: (1) sampling, sample size, and recruitment of participants; (2) data collection techniques; (3) interview questionnaire design; (4) data analysis techniques; and (5) validity and reliability of qualitative research.

Figure 3.2: Research process flowchart

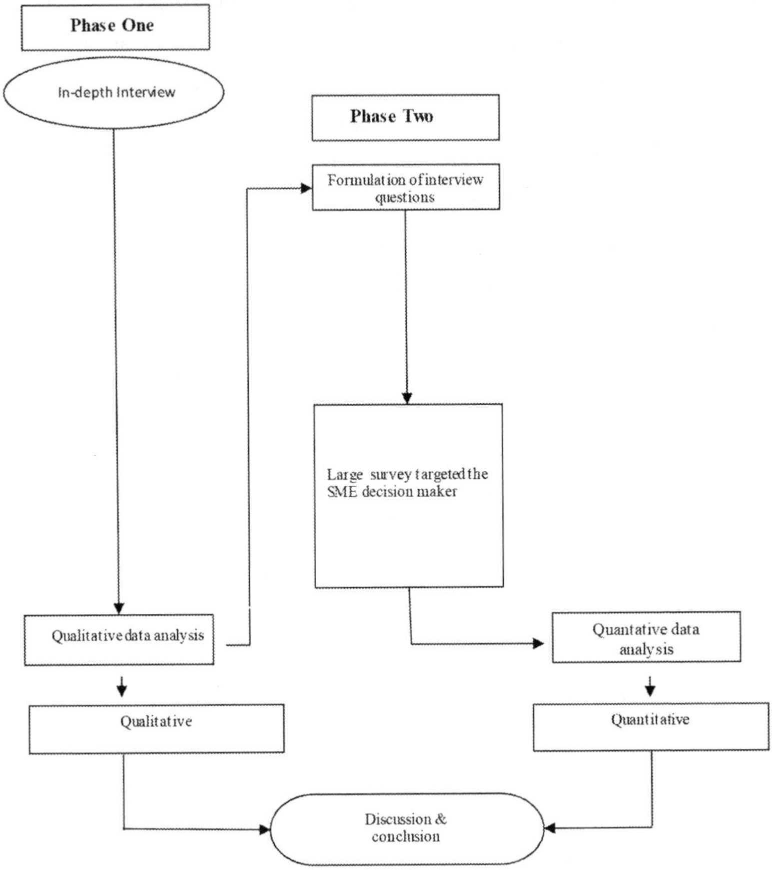

3.2.1 Sampling and sample size

Qualitative studies do not require the sample to be representative of the population as a whole (Creswell, 2003; Neuman, 2003; Thomas, 2008) in the sense of statistical representativeness required for quantitative research. In fact, in qualitative research, there is no general rule for the sample size (Patton, 1990; Marwan, 2010). Instead, the concept of sampling in qualitative studies is to purposefully select specific subjects to examine in order to gain deeper understandings of the defined issues (Creswell, 2003). Eisenhardt (1989, p. 585) suggests that the number of case in qualitative study is ideally between 4 and 10 cases, taking into consideration the constraints of time and funding for postgraduate research (Perry, 1998). The key issue in sampling for qualitative research is not absolute number of respondent but whether the theoretical model saturation has been achieved after respondent X. Thomas (2008) recommends that when the themes and issues in which the researcher is interested become "saturated", meaning that no new data are found from the participation of additional case-firms, no further cases should be approached and the process of data collection should come to end. In other words, the sample size is deemed sufficient when additional fieldwork appears unlikely to change the developed framework significantly (Strauss & Corbin, 1998).

In the qualitative phase of this research, the Organisation A was first identified to conduct the case study. It was then determined that a second case organisation, Organisation B was necessary for comparative reasons. When these two organisations were completed, the Organisation C was chosen to provide further depth to the data. The organisation D was approached to further validate data from organisation A, B, and C. In the end of the interview with organisation D, no significantly new data appeared to be emerging, and thus this phase of the research was completed at this point.

3.2.2 Recruitment of Participants

In qualitative phase, it is important to find the "right person" to be interviewed, as this will determine whether valuable information can be obtained during the interview process. Rubin and Rubin (2005, p. 64) argue that "interviewees should be experienced and knowledgeable in the area you are interviewing about." Experienced interviewees can make the interview results more convincing, and interviewees who are knowledgeable about the research problem have the potential to provide useful information needed (Rubin &

Rubin, 2005). As the objective of the research was to investigate the process of making marketing decision in SME, ideally the respondent should be a decision maker in SME organisation which typically the SME owner manager. In the first step, the list of potential respondents was screened from SMEs list that could add further value to the investigation. The potential respondents were then contact to confirm their participation. During the call screen, the respondents were screened on whether they had business relationship, whether marketing decision making was driven from this business relationship, and whether they were the decision makers of the company.

A few problems were encountered in the initial recruitment of participants for the study. Although the researcher had contacted 20 potential participants from various types of industry, only four SMEs agreed finally to participate in this research. These SMEs were mainly from transportation and trading sectors, which were more approachable compared to other sectors. The potential participants were contacted directly by telephone, and were screened to determine whether they were the decision makers of the organisation.

Appointments were made within a week following the telephone call so that the participants' interest would be sustained and thus they would not forget their appointments.

3.2.3   Qualitative Data Collection Techniques

It is important to understand the theory of qualitative data collection techniques before designing the interview questionnaire. Figure 3.2 shows that data collection techniques for qualitative research can be classified into three major types, interviews, observations, and examining other documents (Wolcott, 2001; Patton, 2002). Two types of personal interviews, in-depth interviews (face-to-face) and telephone interviews are commonly used in qualitative data collection (McLennan, 1999; Zikmund, 2000). In this study, the in-depth interview was a more appropriate data collection method than telephone interview to elicit information from the SMEs owner managers because the nature of the questions was complex and there were many of them. This notion coincides with McLennan's finding (1999) that "it is difficult to obtain detailed answers to complex questions by telephone or mail survey, whereas personal face-to-face interviews will generally yield a greater depth of response." Therefore, the researcher undertook in-depth interviews (face-to-face) using a tape recorder and by taking notes for data collection.

Patton (2002) also describes five interview types as follows: informal conversation, general guided approach, standardised open-ended, closed fixed-response, and combined approach. Patton emphasises that researchers need to keep in mind that all five types of interviewing techniques described above are pure types. In practice, researchers may employ all those techniques or combine several techniques. Informal interviews collect information from informal conversations, while general guided approach follows basic, pre-determined lines of enquiry. Standardised open-ended interviews follow set questions in the same order for each interviewee. Closed fixed-response interviews are suited to questionnaires, and determine categories in advance for respondents to select.

Informal conversational interview techniques were not employed in this present study because data analysis can be difficult to consolidate. Patton (2002) explains that the use of these techniques demands much time to sort through the data, because the questions change over time as each new interview creates new issue from the previous answers. A close-fixed technique was also dropped in this study because the respondents must fit their experiences and feelings into the researcher's categories, which limited their original ideas. Consequently, the approach used in this study was standardised open-ended technique only. Patton (2002) emphasises that this technique is suitable for students and amateur interviewers. This technique also makes data analysis easy, and facilitates gathering and comparison of results as every respondent answers the same questions.

3.2.3.1 In-depth interview

In-depth interview is a powerful method for qualitative data collection because it allows individual interaction between researcher and interviewee, and unclear questions can be clarified immediately (Tashakkori & Teddlie, 1998). In addition, the interview technique allows researchers to explain, gather, and find out the understanding of the interviewees (Patton, 2002). However, only a small number of interviews could be conducted in this study because of the time-consuming nature of this research technique, and due to the expense the interviewees had to sacrifice. The interviews with the SMEs owner managers in this study were aimed at identifying the particular variables or factors that affected the process of making marketing decision. These variables or factors were intended to be compared with the results of the survey questionnaire. Data on the general background of the SMEs owners, including their opinions about process, were also gathered by means of the interviews.

The interviews with the four organisations (Organisation A, B, C, and D) began by gaining informed consent as a part of the ethics approval process (Appendix A). Each participant signed a consent form stating that they understood they could withdraw from the research at any time, and they had received an assurance that all information collected would remain confidential. Interviews were recorded digitally, and were later transcribed manually to give the researcher the closeness to the data, and to allow the theme to emerge (Creswell, 2005). As Creswell (2005) points out, analysing by hand is possible where there are only a small number of transcripts and where the researcher has time to commit to the process in order to achieve this intimate understanding of the emerging themes. The transcripts were prepared with large margins in order for the researcher to take note and identify the theme throughout the document for ready reference during the analysis.

Figure 3.3: Data collection technique for qualitative method

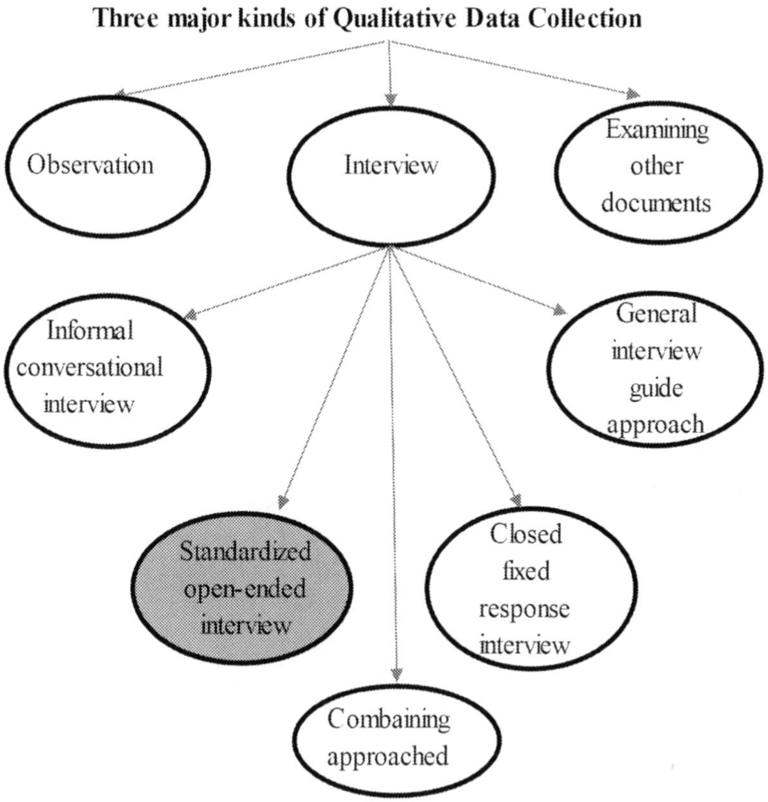

Three major kinds of Qualitative Data Collection

Source: Patton (2002)

3.2.4   Interview Questionnaire Design

At Phase One, the researcher aimed to further extend the emerging issues relating to making marketing decision by the SMEs. The use of in-depth interview was identified as an appropriate data collection method. The question used in the interview process emerged from the literature and conceptual framework. The question used during the interview process is attached as Appendix B. The interview questionnaire used in this study focused on standardised open-ended questions. The standardised open-ended interview technique consists of a set of questions carefully worded and arranged with the intention of taking each respondent through the same sequence, and of asking each respondent the same questions with essentially the same words (Patton, 2002). The questions were determined and worded in a completely open-ended format in advance. The advantages of this technique in the construction of the interview questionnaire have been discussed in the previous section.

The interview questionnaire comprised five main parts (A-E). Part A contained questions aimed at eliciting SMEs owner managers' opinions about the decision method used in the process. Part B and Part C focused on the opinions of the SMEs owners in relation to sources of information and driving factor. Part D questions were designed to elicit the opinions of the SMEs owner managers about the decision outcome in relation to the decision method.

Prior to using this interview questionnaire to elicit information from the SMEs owner managers, it was pre-tested and vetted by industrial experts, i.e., SME Corporation officer, MARA, and Associate Professor of public university specialised in marketing. The results of the pre-test revealed that the questionnaire was understandable for the respondents. Lastly, Part E covered general questions about the background of the SMEs owner managers.

3.2.5 Qualitative Data Analysis Techniques

The methods of qualitative data analysis used in this study was drawn from Miles and Huberman (1984; 1994) who propose three phases that can be applied to within and cross-case analyses of the qualitative data. This methodology involves the following phases:

- Data reduction
- Data display
- Conclusion drawing and verification

Data reduction implies organising and reducing a large volume of collected qualitative data and field notes. It also refers to the course of selecting, focusing, simplifying, summarising, and converting the data of written field notes and the transcript interview. As a major element of this phase, the data require summarising and coding, and finally categories and themes need to be created according to predetermined research question. Coding refers to tag or label for assigning units of meaning to the descriptive or inferential information compiled during a study. Coding can be performed through using numerical or written codes to categorise certain portions of data that match different themes (Lacey & Luff, 2001). The identified research question and research conceptual framework represent principle guideline for the data analysis as the researcher has to search for answer to the research question within the data (Moione, 1997).

Data display as a second phase entails presenting the reduced data in organised and understandable shape to allow the researcher to reach conclusion about the research issue. According to Miles & Huberman (1984, p. 21), "all displays are designed to assemble and organize information in an immediately accessible, compact form, so that the analyst can see what is happening and either draw justified conclusion or move on the next step analysis which the display suggests may useful." Word or diagrammatic form such flow charts, table, and other graphics can be used to assemble and systematise the information. In addition, a matrix can be applied for analysing patterns of responses to the research question.

Conclusion drawing and verification as the final phase of the three-phase data analysis methodology are also known as the interpretation phase (Creswell, 1994; Wolcott, 1990). This phase implies giving meaning and sense to the analysed data through searching for descriptive patterns in the data. According to the Miles & Huberman (1994), drawing conclusion means simply recognising the meanings of the analysed data and evaluating the implications of these meanings, while verifying refers to the meanings emerging from the data that have to be tested for their sturdiness and conformability, that is, their validity.

In conclusion, within-case and cross-case analyses were carried out in analysing the data of the current research. The case study description, report, or story was used as an analytic strategy for within-case analysis due to its wide deployment in previous strategic decision making research. Furthermore, the pattern or theme matching was compared with the emerged themes with patterns derived from the literature review.

In cross-case analysis, the case studies were categorised based on the size and type of industry such as large firms vs. small firm, and followed by search for similarities and differences among these categories. Analytic strategy was adopted to find the cross-case patterns (Eisenhardt, 1989). Furthermore, the three-phase data analysis methodology (Miles & Huberman, 1984; 1994) was employed in analysing the data of the case studies. The procedures of the data analysis are discussed in the next section.

3.2.5.1 Data Analysis Procedure

The within-case analysis was performed first followed by cross-case analysis involving analysing the data of each case study independently, collected mainly via in-depth interviews. Once the within-case analysis for the four case studies was completed, a cross-case analysis was carried out by using the formerly discussed strategies. The main procedures incorporated in within-case analysis process are as follows:

First phase: All the interviews were recorded during the interview sessions using a recording device.

Second phase: The recorded interviews were manually transcribed verbatim. Each interview was ranged from 1 hour to almost 2 hours.

Third phase: Prior commencing analysis of data, the author consulted doctoral colleague who had carried out research using qualitative data. In addition, the author reviewed handbook sources in relation to qualitative data analysis.

Fourth phase: The researcher listened carefully to the tape interviews more than once, read the interview transcriptions thoroughly, and listened again to the key ideas and themes captured, which were linked to the main research question (Swallow, Newton & Van Lottum, 2002). The field notes taken during the site visits to the participating SMEs were very valuable and necessary in assisting the author in the preliminary identification for the anticipated main themes about the process of making the marketing decision.

Fifth phase: A report was created for each case study as the focal point of within-case analysis by combining the interviews into narrative (story style). The case study report (as shown in Chapter 4) included several themes that described the main SME managerial procedures as well as critical success factors involved in the process of making marketing decision. These themes were developed by utilising the process of data reduction and display, whereas the process of drawing conclusion and verifications was employed following the cross-case analysis. The data reduction process began with coding or indexing the data of interview transcription into categories and consequently, abbreviated codes of few letters were assigned for emerging themes or pattern to assist in organising the data into categories. Subsequently, core categories for the emerging themes and patterns were established, and descriptive label was given to each category. The categories were defined after working on the data as a result of the data reduction stage, and broken into subcategories when appropriate.

As a result, the core categories represented the main phases of the process in making marketing decision, while the subcategories represented the factors, attributes, and elements of each main decision phase. Afterwards, the data of within-case-case analysis were displayed using texts and tables. Initially, the author began by displaying each core category and subcategory separately by using texts and tables, and ended by displaying the theme reflecting the research questions through of case summary tables for each case. Later, these summary tables were utilised in the cross-case analysis. Moreover, in the cross-case analysis, the relevant findings of the four case studies were displayed by using a matrix to capture the similarities and differences among the cases.

Sixth phase: Finally, the process of interpretation and conclusion drawing and its verification were undertaken to complete the cross-case analysis. Conclusion drawing is discussed in Chapter 4, and it implied attaching meaning, sense, and significance to the cross-case analysis and findings. Verification or validity is explained in detail in the next section, and involved re-examining and revising the analysed data as required in order to verify and confirm the emerging conclusion.

In brief, the within and cross-case analyses and results are explained in detail and displayed in the next chapter. The sample of the adopted data analysis methodology during the analysis course of the current research is provided in Appendix B.

3.2.6 Validity and reliability of the interview questionnaire

In terms of validity and reliability of qualitative data used in this study, no absolute formula for determining significance was available in the same way as for the measurement of quantitative data. Therefore, in accordance with Patton (2002), the results were presented in relation to the purpose of the study. Validity was achieved through interpretation, and reliability was observed through significant agreement between respondents (Kirk & Miller, 1986).

Wolcot (1994) emphasises that qualitative researchers need to focus their work on objectivity, reliability, validity, or replicability, and to "stay descriptive as long as possible." According to Patton (2002), "the strategy of triangulating with multiple data sources, observations, methods, and/or theories, researcher can make substantial strides in overcoming the scepticism that greets singular methods, lone analysis, and single-perspective interpretations." Tashakkori and Teddlie (1998) point out that triangulation methods often involve comparing and integrating data collected through qualitative research with data collected through some kind of quantitative study. This practical approach of mixed methods analysis assumes potential compatibility, and seeks to discover the degree and nature of compatibility, which were part of this research. Validity and reliability of the quantitative aspects of this research are discussed in quantitative section.

3.3   Phase 2: Quantitative Phase

Phase Two was the quantitative component of the research, and involved the development, administration, and analysis of a survey questionnaire. The instrument was developed based upon the results of Phase One, in order to provide an initial test of the process model that emerged from that phase. Creswell *et al.* (2003) emphasise that it is important to allow the findings of the qualitative phase to inform the quantitative stage, with necessary changes to the quantitative stage being made following analysis of the qualitative stage. Therefore, the objective of Phase Two was to better understand the process and the element involved in the making marketing decision process from the large survey. The specific details of instrument development, case and participant selection, data collection and analysis are detailed below.

3.3.1 Survey Instrument Development

Design of survey questionnaire is critical for an effective research, and three issues have been highlighted as important in this process, namely question wording, categorisation and coding of the variable, and general appearance (Sekaran, 2003). Each of these issues was considered in the development of the survey questionnaire for Phase Two. The wording was specifically developed based in the wording outcomes from Phase One, and external panel was consulted for additional quality checks. The categorisation of variable was done prior to the instrument development by careful planning of analysis around research questions. Finally, the appearance was assessed by the use of the expert panel, as an integral part of the pilot study.

3.3.1.1 Survey questionnaire construction

The survey instrument that was developed for Phase Two comprised five sections (Appendix C).The first five sections (A, B, C, D, E) were developed from the outcomes of Phase One, and presented with statement to which participants responded using selection answer and Likert scales. These sections of the survey will be referred as Decision Method (Section A), Source of Information (Section B), Driving factor (Section C), and Decision Outcome (Section D). The process of development of the statement will be outlined in the next section of the chapter.

The final section of the survey (Section E) was demographic data relating to the decision makers, including age, gender, ethnicity, and qualification. This information was collected as nominal data, and specific rationale was used to develop the groupings. For example, the age of decision maker identified corresponded with the effectiveness of decision (Heck, Rowe, & Owen, 1995). Also gathered in this section was about decision makers' length of tenure in the current organisation, and specifically in their current position. As discussed in the literature review, the decision makers accumulate both explicit and tacit knowledge over time. Therefore, the length of time for the decision makers in their position could be used as an indicator of experience and provided some insight into depth and knowledge.

3.3.1.2 Scales selection

Four major types of scales namely nominal, ordinal, interval, and ratio are widely used for measurement of response options in marketing research, and also in social and behavioural sciences (Hester, 1996; Tashakkori & Teddlie, 1998; Zikmund, 2000; Sekaran, 2000; DeVellis, 2003). In this current study, nominal measures were used to classify characteristics of respondents, while ordinal and interval measures were used to measure respondents' opinions about marketing decision. Ratio measure is similar to interval measure, differing only in the use of a zero point (Hester, 1996; Tashakkori & Teddlie, 1998). But, in this study, as an absolute zero, ratio measures were not used.

In designing quantitative questionnaires suitable to investigate attitudes and behaviours results, the widely recommended Likert scale was used as it was easy to prepare and interpret, and it was simple for the respondents to answer (Zikmund, 2000; Sekaran, 2000; Schifftnan, 2001). Other than that, Likert scale has been widely proven to be applicable in diverse applications, and a valid way to accurately measure opinions, beliefs, and attitudes (DeVellis, 2003). A good Likert item should state the opinion, attitude, belief, or other construct under study in clear terms. DeVellis (2003) notes that, "When a Likert scale is used, the item is presented as a declarative sentence, followed by response options that indicate varying degrees of agreement with or endorsement of the statement."

Overall length of scales, labelling, and balancing are the three most controversial issues when choosing response scales (Darbyshire & McDonald, 2004). It is also claimed that scales with only labelled end points provide flexibility for analysis as long as respondents can understand the meaning of the scale (Darbyshire & McDonald, 2004). Research has also shown that longer scales often have no more reliability than those that are shorter, for example 11 points versus 5 points (Darbyshire & McDonald, 2004). In choosing the most appropriate response scale, the researcher adopted guidelines from Kivela (2000), who used five-point scale with labelled end points that would be able to be understood by respondents. However, they should be given the opportunity for a neutral response by the provision of a mid-point.

3.3.1.3 Development of Survey Questionnaire Statements

The statements in Phase Two survey were developed to reflect findings from the first phase of the study, and were developed around the constructs present in the process model resulting from Phase One (Appendix D). Where possible, the item developed as a result of Phase One used verbatim comments or common phrasing from Phase One to ensure the appropriateness of wording. The developed statement was subject to pretesting by an expert panel. The pretest was done to address tautological issues, to clarify statements, and to ensure that the instrument would address the research questions in an appropriate manner (Sigh & Smith, 2000). It is also acknowledged that use of pretest contributed to the overall reliability and validity of the instrument (McClelland, 1994), something which would be examined in further detail in a subsequent section of this chapter. The expert panel consisted of SME Corp, MARA officer, and candidate for Doctor of Philosophy (Ph.D) from University of Melbourne, Australia.

3.3.2　Refining the Survey Questionnaire

McLennan (1999) points out that the process of testing is an important part of preparing and developing the survey questionnaire because problems can be identified and corrected before the full survey is conducted. Three main types of testing techniques namely observational studies, pre-testing, and pilot testing can be used for developing the survey questionnaire (McLennan, 1999).

3.3.2.1 Observational studies technique

In this current research, the observational studies technique, adapted from McLennan (1999), was used for developing the questionnaire during pretesting and pilot testing stages. Respondents were required to complete the second draft questionnaire in the presence of an observer. While completing the questionnaire, respondents were asked to explain their understanding of the questions. Respondents were informed that the questionnaire was being pilot-tested, and that it was not part of the actual survey. The researcher was also careful to ensure that the respondents were not given any assistance in completing the questionnaire. Observational studies help to identify problem questions, questions likely to be asked by the respondents, and the time taken to complete the questionnaire. More opinions and comments were elicited from the respondents during observations at the pretesting and pilot testing stages.

3.3.2.2 Pretesting technique

According to Zikmund (2000), "pre-testing a questionnaire on a small sample of respondents is a useful way to discover problems while they still can be corrected." Therefore, the first pretest of the questionnaire was an informal test with a total of four respondents. The questionnaire was self-administered, and after completion, the respondents were asked some questions in order to obtain their feedback about the questionnaire. Pretesting was carried out to screen out problems in the design of the questionnaire, and to identify ambiguous questions and respondent misunderstanding, that is, whether the questions meant the same thing to all respondents (Zikmund, 2000). Qualitative questions were also used at the first pretesting stage, asking respondents for more variables that affected them in getting to know about the decision process.

Results showed that majority of the pilot respondents complained that there were too many items to answer, which they found to be boring and time-consuming. They just ticked the appropriate box and mentioned that they were not sure whether the questions were about the marketing decision making process. The revised questions were reformatted to ensure that all questions were related to the proposed model and were understandable to respondents before the launch of the questionnaire for pilot testing.

3.3.2.3 Pilot testing technique

Pilot testing is used to formally test a survey questionnaire with a small sample of respondents similar to those in the final survey in order to maximise the validity of the results, and to ensure that consequent modifications to the survey questionnaire are appropriate (McLennan, 1999; Zikmund, 2000; Pallant, 2002; Nardi, 2003).

After the modification of pretest questionnaire, the pilot test questionnaire was commented by industry experts, i.e., SME Corp, MARA officer, and candidate for Doctor of Philosophy (Ph.D) from University of Melbourne, Australia to ensure that respondents could understand the questions, the order of questions flowed in a logical sequence, wording of questions and format were clear, and time taken to answer the questions was reasonable (McLennan, 1999; Zikmund, 2000; Pallant, 2002; Nardi, 2003). The pilot testing technique was also used to confirm the validity and reliability of the questionnaire, including information on the design, layout, wording, and measurement scales (Kivela, 1999).

In this study, the questionnaires were distributed to 50 respondents from various industries. However, only 14 respondents completed the survey for analysis.

3.3.3   Findings of the Pilot Test Study

Useful data were gathered at the pilot-tested questionnaire stage. During data collection on the spot, respondents were asked whether they understood all questions after completing the questionnaires. As all participants understood the questions, results confirmed that the pilot-tested questionnaire was more understandable to respondents than the earlier pretested questionnaires.

3.3.4 Data Analysis for Pilot Test

The purpose of data analysis for the pilot test data stage was to use samples to check the reliability of the questionnaire before launching the actual survey for this study. Data from the completed questionnaires collected from 14 respondents were entered into the SPSS program for screening and cleaning the data using the three steps suggested by Pallant (2002), namely checking for errors, finding the errors in the data file, and correcting the errors in the data file references. Data were examined for the frequencies for each of the items and all of the individual items and the scales to check for errors. Two ways were used at the pilot test stage: frequency statistics, which was used for checking categorical items; and descriptive statistics, which was used for checking continuous items (Pallant, 2002). Reliability was also investigated at this stage. Results were used to compare with reliability of the actual survey questionnaire. The 14 respondents of the pilot-tested study were excluded from the actual survey for this study. Sampling, sample size, and ways for recruitment of participants are discussed in next section.

3.4 Phase Two Sampling, Sample Size, and Recruitment of Participants

This section consists of three main parts: sampling and sample size of the targeted population for this study, the strategy for recruitment of participants for increasing the response rate, and the response rate itself.

3.4.1 Sampling

In this study, nonprobability sampling was used as it was appropriate for exploratory research. Lists of SMEs registered in the Malaysian SMEs business directory were drawn, and 500 respondents were randomly chosen from various industries to distribute the questionnaire. The targeted population was decision makers responsible for making marketing decision.

3.4.2 Sample size

The targeted respondent was calculated from the formula that five respondents for each item in the questionnaire are enough in most cases (Tabachnick & Fidell, 2001). In this study, the total of 36 items in the survey questionnaire was multiplied by five respondents for each item. Consequently, at least 180 respondents were needed to collect enough data for inferential analysis.

3.4.3 Recruitment of participants

The strategy for recruitment of the participant started with enlisting the personal contact of SMEs registered in Malaysian SMEs business directory. These personnel were mostly the owner managers or marketing managers of SME Company. To ensure this respondent provided valid and reliable insight into business-to-business marketing decision making, the researcher had followed up with telephone call with these key informants.

3.4.4 Types of data analysis techniques

Statistics for data analysis are classified into two main types namely descriptive and inferential (Zikmund, 2000; Tabachnick & Fidell, 2001; Kerr *et al.*, 2002; Antonius, 2003). Descriptive statistics attempt to summarise observations and experience (Rowntree, 1981), or to describe samples of subjects in terms of variables or combinations of variables (Tabachnick & Fidell, 2001). Inferential statistics use those observations as a basis for making estimates or predictions about what is likely to happen in the future (Rowntree, 1981), or to "test hypotheses about differences in populations on the basis of measurements made on samples of subjects" (Tabachnick & Fidell, 2001). The distinction between descriptive and inferential statistics depends upon samples and populations (Rowntree, 1981). According to Tabachnick and Fidell (2001), descriptive statistics are used to provide estimations of central tendency and the like in the population if reliable differences are found. These measurements are called "parameter estimates". Generally, researchers are interested in both descriptive and inferential statistics to analyse their data. Many assumptions of multivariate statistical methods are used only for inferential analysis. However, there are more limitations on inferential analysis than on descriptive analysis (Tabachnick & Fidell, 2001).

According to Tashakkori and Teddlie (1998), descriptive statistics, graphs, or combination of the two is not sufficient for most research purposes, particularly for estimation and testing of hypotheses. Testing of hypotheses is based on estimations of how much error is involved in obtaining a difference between groups, or a relationship between variables. In this study, descriptive statistics included presentations of results through simple statistics and graphic displays. The main objective of these analyses was to provide images and/or summaries that can help the reader understand the nature of the variables and their relationship.

The present study employed a commonly used method for descriptive data analysis and presentation:, i.e., measures of central tendency, which summarise a group of observation or scores into a single score. Tashakkori and Teddlie (1998) also explain that mode, mean, and median are all measures of central tendency, and are single scores that represent groups of events/people. Mode is the most frequent score in a group. Mode can be calculated for variables that are measured on nominal scales. Mean in the average of scores (sum divided by number of scores). In other words, mean is the average of all scores in the distribution. Mean contains information regarding all members of the group. Mean is used to measure an ordinal or higher (interval or ration) scale. Median is the score at or below which 50% of the scores fall (it divides the group or score into two equal halves). In other words, median is the score in the middle of distribution. Median is used to measure ordinal (rank order) scale.

It is important to understand the type of scales for measurement before choosing which statistics are suitable for data analysis. In analysis of this study, all the three types of scale namely nominal, ordinal, and interval were used for measurement (Tashakkori & Teddle, 1998: Zikmund, 2000; Antonious, 2003). In reporting results for questions in the interview questionnaire and the survey questionnaire, frequencies, percentages, mean, median, mode, and standard deviation were used for descriptive analysis.

Because descriptive analysis was not suitable to test the hypotheses in this study, inferential statistics were used. Tashakkori and Teddlie (1998) and Pallant (2005) classify statistical techniques into two major means of finding results: to explore differences between/among groups, and to explore relationships between/among variables. Tashakkori and Teddlie (1998) develop "The Quantitative Data Analysis Matrix" for gaining inferential statistics. They maintain that there are two ways to find out results for testing hypotheses: results for "differences between groups", and results for "relationship between variables". In this study, when results for "differences between groups" were required, in agreement with Tashakkori and Teddlie (1998), an analysis of variance (ANOVA) was used for interval/ordinal data. When the results for "relationship between variables" were required, then Pearson correlation and multiple regression analysis were used for interval/ordinal data.

Analysis of Variance (ANOVA)

ANOVA analysis was suitable for testing the null hypotheses Ho1 to Ho11, because it is a hypothesis-testing procedure that is used to evaluate mean differences between two or more populations (called independent variables) and one dependent variable (Gravetter & Wallnau, 2004). These eleven null hypotheses were aimed to at finding out the significant differences between independent variable and dependent variable.

Antonius (2003) and Gravetter and Wallnau (2004) emphasise that ANOVA is similar to a *t*-test, but ANOVA is used for two or more groups, while *t*-test is used for two groups. The *t*-test as a procedure of hypothesis testing is more appropriate when the sample is small (less than or equal to 30 individuals), but it can also be used for large samples, as the *t* distribution looks increasingly like a normal distribution as the number of respondents grows larger (Antonius, 2003). In addition, Gravetter and Wallnau (2004) highlight that both ANOVA and *t*-tests "are simply two different ways of doing exactly the same job" of using sample data to test hypotheses about populations for mean differences. Thus, in this study, ANOVA was used for testing the mean significant differences for two and more groups in this study because "ANOVA has a tremendous advantage over *t*-tests," and it provided the researcher with great flexibility in designing experiments and interpreting results (Gravetter & Wallnau, 2004).

Three main types of analysis of variance (ANOVA) that can be used for testing hypotheses are one-way ANOVA between-groups, two-way between-groups ANOVA, and mixed between-within subjects ANOVA (Pallant, 2002; 2005). In this present study, one-way ANOVA was used to test the null hypotheses Ho3 to Ho10 because there were one independent variable and one dependent variable. Two-way between-groups ANOVA and mixed between-within subjects ANOVA were not used for testing the hypotheses in this study because independent variables were not suitable to this type of ANOVA analysis.

Therefore, using the SPSS program in accordance with Pallant (2005), five major tests of an ANOVA analysis were used for evaluating the results of the null hypotheses including:

i. Test of Homogeneity of Variances is used for testing whether the variance in scores is the same for each of three groups.

A significance value of Levene's test of more than .05 indicates that the assumption of homogeneity of variance is not violated. This means that the significance value of ANOVA ($p<.05$) using Test of Between-Subjective Effects can be used to interpret results in terms of the significant difference for the mean scores on the dependent variable for between or among groups. However, if Levene's test finds that the assumption of homogeneity of variance is violated ($p<.05$), an alternative test using Robust Tests of Equality of Means (Welsh and Brown-Forsythe) is recommended.

ii. Test of Between-Subjects Effects (ANOVA) provides between-groups and within-groups sums of squares, degrees of freedom (df), a significant F test, a significance value (p), and partial eta squared. F ratio, which represents the variance between the groups, is calculated, and divided by the variance within the significant F test means that the null hypothesis can be rejected, which states that the population means are equal. A significance value of less than or equal to .01 means that there is a significant difference among the mean scores on the dependent variable among groups. Nonetheless, the significance value does not tell which group is different from another group. A large F ratio indicates that there is more variability between the groups.

iii. The Post-hoc Multiple Comparisons Test using Tukey HSD is used for measuring exactly where the differences are among the groups. Post-hoc comparisons with an appropriate alpha level of .01 have also been designed to protect against the possibility of an increased type 1 error. A significance value of less than or equal to .01 was used in this study to indicate that the two groups being compared were significantly different from one another.

iv. Test of Mean Differences provides information about the number of respondents in each group, means, and standard deviation.

v. Lastly, partial eta squared value (eta squared) is used for evaluating the actual differences in the mean scores of groups.

$$\text{Eta squared} = \frac{\text{Sum of squares between-groups}}{\text{Total sum of squares}}$$

In this study, the actual differences in the mean scores of groups were tested by using the partial eta squared (eta squared) value. In agreement with Cohen (1988), results of the eta squared value were classified as .01 for a small effect, .06 for a medium effect, and .14 for a large effect.

Correlation Analysis

Correlation analysis was appropriate for testing the null hypotheses Ho10 in order to answer the Research Question 4 because it was a hypothesis-testing procedure used to evaluate and describe the strength and direction of the linear relationship between two continuous variables. This null hypothesis aimed at finding out the significant relationship between decision method and decision outcome.

Two types of correlation analysis (parametric technique) used in research are bivariate correlation Pearson product-moment coefficient (between two variables) and partial correlation (to explore the relationship between two variables while controlling for another variable). Bivariate correlation Pearson product-moment coefficient is designed to test the significant relationships between two variables with an interval level (continuous) variable. Pearson correlation coefficients (r) can only take on values from –1 to +1. The sign indicates whether there is a positive correlation or a negative correlation. A positive correlation (+1) means that one variable increases, so too does the other. If the correlation between two variables is positive and close to 1, the variables have a strong positive linear correlation. A negative correlation (–1) means that one variable increases, the other decreases. If the correlation between two variables is negative and close to –1, the variables have a strong negative linear correlation. Interpretation of the value of Pearson correlation used in this study followed the guidelines from Cohen (1988) as a correlation of r = 0 indicates no relationship at all; a correlation of r = 1.0 indicates a perfect positive correlation; a correlation of r = –1.0 indicates a perfect negative correlation; a correlation of r = .10 to .29 or r = –.10 to .29 indicates a small correlation; a correlation of r = .30 to .49 or r = –.30 to –.49 indicates a medium correlation; a correlation of r = .50 to 1.0 or r = –.50 to –1.0 indicates a large correlation. Correlation analysis was used to test Ho11.

T-Test Analysis

The independent-samples t test evaluates the difference between the means of two independent or unrelated groups. That is, we evaluate whether the means for two independent groups are significantly different from each other. The independent-samples t test is commonly referred to as a between-groups design, and can also be used to analyze a control and experimental group. With an independent-samples t test, each case must have scores on two variables, the grouping (independent) variable and the test (dependent) variable. The grouping variable divides cases into two mutually exclusive groups or categories, such as male or female for the grouping variable gender, while the test variable describes each case on some quantitative dimension such as test performance. The t test evaluates whether the mean value of the test variable (e.g., test performance) for one group (e.g., male) differs significantly from the mean value of the test variable for the second group (e.g. female). In this study, T-Test analysis was used to test Ho2.

Multiple Regression Analysis

There are three types of multiple regression analysis namely standard, hierarchical, and stepwise (Pallant, 2005). Standard multiple regression is commonly used for entering all the independent/predictor variables into the equation at the same time. Each independent variable is evaluated in terms of its predictive power, over and above, offered by all other independent variables. In hierarchical regression, the independent variables are entered into equation in order specified by the researcher, based on theoretical grounds. In stepwise regression, the researcher provides SPSS is provided with a list of independent variables, and then the program is allowed to select which variables it will enter, and in which order they go into the equation, based on a set of statistical criteria. There are three versions of this approach namely forward selection, backward detention, and stepwise regression. In this study, standard multiple regression analysis was chosen as appropriate for testing the null hypotheses Ho1 because it is a hypothesis-testing procedure used to explore the relationship between one continuous dependent variable and a number of continuous independent variable/predictors (Pallant, 2005). In this study, the null hypothesis Ho1 was aimed at investigating which of the twelve independent variables of driving factors was the best for predicting the decision outcome.

3.5   Valid and Missing Data in Survey Questionnaire Responses

"Valid data" refer to answered questions, and "missing data" refer to unanswered questions in the questionnaire. In analysing the significance of both validated and missed answers, two methods were selected in this study, namely "exclude cases pairwise" and "exclude cases list wise" (Pallant, 2002; 2005). The option of "exclude cases pairwise" was used for descriptive analysis. In this method, responses were only excluded when necessary information had been omitted. The "exclude cases list wise" option was used for the inferential because it provides the same number of responses for every item in each question. In this method, responses are omitted when there are missing variables, so it can limit sample size because it deletes all respondents, even when only one item is missing. However, this method was still suitable for use in this study because there was adequate number of respondents, and there was a low percentage of missing responses for each item. Consequently, there was no problem of a limited sample size for this study. In accordance with Pallant (2002; 2005), the "replace with mean" technique was not used in this study because it has the potential of severely distorting the results of analysis.

3.5.1 Validity of survey questionnaire

In this study, the Statistical Package for Social Sciences (SPSS) version 18.0 was employed to evaluate the construct validity and reliability of the survey questionnaire. Validity tests of the questionnaire were performed to ensure that the questions measured the right concept, while reliability tests were used to test the stability and consistency of the questionnaire items, using interval scales for their measurement (Sekaran, 2000). Validity is discussed in this section, while reliability is explained in following section.

Sekaran (2000) emphasises that reliability is necessary but it is an insufficient measure of the quality of the questionnaire. A measure of responses may establish a high stability and consistency but may not be the concept that one sets out to measure. The questionnaire needs to be tested for validity in order to ensure the ability of the scales to measure the intended concept of this present study. In this study, two types of validity test namely content validity and construct validity were used to test the validity of the survey questionnaire (Sekaran, 2000; Zikmund, 2000; Nardi, 2003). The criterion-related validity technique was not applicable as respondents were not selected on the basis of their difference.

3.5.1.1 Content validity

In order to ensure that the survey questionnaire covered all items for the measurement of a concept for this study, content validity in the formulation of questionnaire was obtained in three stages namely observational studies, pretesting, and pilot testing techniques (McLennan, 1999). Firstly, the observational studies technique was used to observe and elicit opinions and comments from respondents during their completion of the questionnaire at both pretesting and pilot stage. Secondly, the questionnaire was pretested. This stage aimed to ensure that the questions were clear and understandable to respondents, and provided suitable answers (Zimund, 2000). Furthermore, the questionnaire was also pretested by experts who had Ph.D degree in marketing areas. They proofread the questionnaire content and gave valuable feedback on simplification of the format and the appropriate number of respondents needed. The purpose of this stage was to ensure that the content of the scale appeared to be adequate and "the measure provides adequate coverage of the concept" (Zikmund, 2000). The survey questionnaire in this study was considered to be content-valid. According to Zikmund (2000) and Sekaran (2000), if the content of the scales and the measure concept are evaluated by a group of professional or expert judges, they will be accurate and adequate. Thirdly, the survey questionnaire was pilot-tested by 14 respondents. This stage focused on two main aims: (1) to measure the content validity of the survey questionnaire with the actual potential respondents before launching the final survey study, and (2) to measure the reliability of questions (interval scales) by using Cronbach's alpha technique.

3.5.1.2 Reliability of the Survey Questionnaire Responses

There are four major methods used for evaluating reliability of the responses, namely test-retest, parallel-form, internal consistency, and split-half (Sekaran, 2000; Zikmund, 2000; Nardi, 2003). Both test-retest and parallel-form methods are established by testing for stability reliability. The test-retest method was not appropriate for measurement of reliability in this study because the nature of the data collection method, i.e., involving different respondents at different locations, making it impossible to administer the same questionnaire to the same respondents at two separate times to test for stability, as this method requires. In addition, Zikmund (2000) emphasises that problems that may occur with the measures of test-retest method, as results from the second test may be influenced by the results of the first test, and respondents' attitude may be changed over the period of time. The parallel-form reliability method was also not selected as a test for use in this study because it requires the use of two alternative questionnaires (similar items and the same response format with only the wordings and the ordering of questions changed) with the same respondents at two different times (Sekaran, 2000).

Another two methods (split-half and internal consistency) are established by testing for consistency reliability (Sekaran, 2000). The split-half reliability method is suited for checking internal consistency when there are a large number of items in one question. This method was not employed in this study because the results of reliability may diversify, as it depended on how to split the items into two halves (Sekaran, 2000).

Therefore, the internal consistency reliability method was considered the most appropriate for this present study because it allowed the use of Cronbach's alpha to test the consistency of respondents' answers to all the items in a measure (Sekaran, 2000). Cronbach's alpha measures the internal consistency reliability for multipoint-scaled items, and indicates how well the items in a set of questionnaire are positively correlated to one another, including how well they fit together as a set. In this case, the reliability of a measure indicates error-free (without bias) data, and offers consistency in measurements across time and the various items in the instrument (Sekaran, 2000).

This test computes in terms of average inter-correlations among items measuring the concept. The closer the Cronbach's alpha coefficient is to 1, the higher is the internal consistency reliability (Sekaran, 2000). A minimum value of .50 for Cronbach's alpha is considered adequate as an indication of reliability (Hair, 1998; Anderson & Black, 1995; Kivela, 1999). In addition, Sekaran (2000) also indicates that, in terms of reliability, when the alpha is less than .60, the reliability is considered to be poor; reliability in the .60 to .70 range is acceptable; and reliability over .80 is good.

Cronbach's alpha statistics were used to test the reliability and internal consistency of each of the items and the scales used in the questionnaire. In this study, seven questions had to be checked for the reliability, and internal consistency of these interval scales were used for measurement. Results for the reliability of the question using Cronbach's alpha for testing are shown in Table 3.1.

Table 3.1: Result of Reliability using Cronbach's alpha

Question No.	Number of item	Number of respondents	Cronbach's alpha
1	2	182	0.659
2	15	182	0.776
3	14	182	0.742
4	4	182	0.874

3.6   Summary

This chapter has presented the research design and methodology of the study. Mixed methods (combining qualitative and quantitative research) were designed for data collection and analysis. Next up, Chapter 4 presents the results of the interviews with four SME decision makers.

CHAPTER 4

QUALITATIVE ANALYSIS

4.0 Introduction

The purpose of this chapter is to discuss the findings obtained from the analysis in the qualitative study addressing the SMEs marketing decision making process. The findings are the results of the data collected via in-depth interviews with four SMEs decision makers. Furthermore, the findings of each case study are comprehensively and individually presented in this chapter because of each case represents an independent information-rich experiment (Stake, 1995; Yin, 2003).

The analyses begin with the profiles and characteristics of the respondents who were also the decision makers of their organisations. These organisations were given some abbreviated codes (letter), and confidential information was not included in the organisation background section as to protect their real identities. The following research issues were examined during the interviews: 1) decision making method; 2) sources of information; 3) driving factors; and 4) decision outcomes.

The key findings of the four research questions are summarised and compared with the conceptual framework process drawn from the literature review. The illustrative quotations of the in-depth interview were provided verbatim throughout the chapter, not merely to illustrate the theme being described and to support the findings of each case, but to provide the voice and experience of the decision makers as straightforward as possible. A process of SMEs marketing decision making is presented to illustrate the finding of each case.

Information gained from these interviews is used to confirm and add to the information obtained from the results of the questionnaire. The similarities and differences found in respondents' opinions are used to compare to the quantitative data, and as a basis for an in-depth understanding of the impact of changes in government funding.

Finally, this chapter presents a cross-case analysis to report the similarities and differences among the four cases conducted in relation to the research question. Matrix and tables are utilised during the cross-case analysis to compare and contrast the theme from within case result. The case findings are combined to answer the research question.

4.1   Case 1: Company A

4.1.1   Company background

Company A is a small firm based in Johor. The company was established in 2005, focusing on construction and transportation business specifically in construction of Ready Mix (RMx) plant and warehousing in Johor. This company owns 20 mixer trucks supplied to Ready Mix operators within Johor Bahru district and a workshop to provide repair and maintenance services.

4.1.2   Company structure

The company office is located at Pasir Gudang Industrial Area, and jointly managed by the owner manager and his wife, whom is also a shareholder of the company. The daily operation of the company is headed by the owner manager, and he is assisted by two operation managers for construction and transportation business. In construction business, the construction works are mainly outsourced to third parties who mostly are the owner manager's close friends.

As such, only a few personnel are employed in this section. Next, in transportation business, there are workshop and fleet operation managed by two supervisors. Organisation chart based on the information given by the owner manager is illustrated in Figure 4.1.

Figure 4.1: Organisation chart of Company A

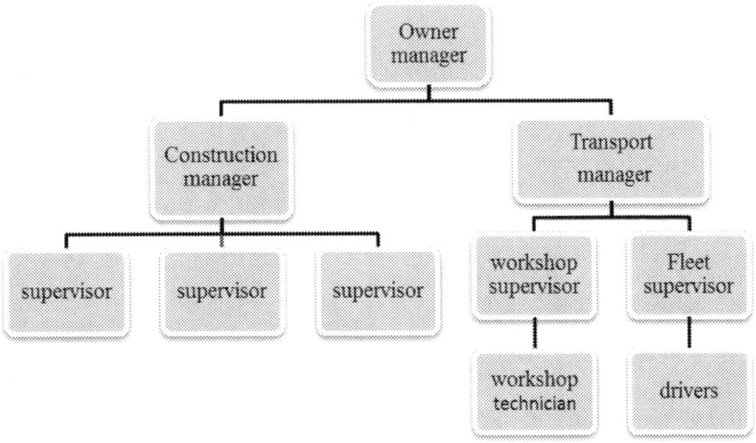

Source: Owner manager of Company A

4.1.3   Interviewee

The interview was conducted at the owner manager's office located in Pasir Gudang. The owner manager is a 45-year old Chinese man. The interview was focused on decision making process specifically related to the marketing decision making processes within the company.

Previously, the owner manager was a supervisor with a small company involved in construction industry. After serving for 20 years, the owner manager decided to resign and set up a small workshop providing service for construction vehicle, i.e., mixer and tipper truck. His wide experience in the construction industry had attracted attention from one MNC company involved in the material building business that intended to use his expertise to involve in their new business channel in the construction industry. This was the first move for a further cooperation in the business. As a result, he was awarded a contract to construct a few new Ready Mix plants and warehousing within Johor Baharu. He had also been appointed as a transporter for these plants. Within a few years, the business had evolved from construction to transportation. The success of this cooperation had drawn attention in the market where a few competitors started to approach the owner manager for collaboration purpose.

4.1.4   Marketing practice in Company A

The marketing practice in Company A is a typical SMEs case where relationship is the focal point in the process. In this case, the owner manager plays a significant role in maintaining a good relationship with a few important key decision makers or potential decision makers mainly the head of department. The owner describes the importance to maintain relationship with these key decision makers:

> "I start develop relationship with these people while I'm still working with my previous company. When I left the company, I still contact them and we are still meet up after the office hour for tea. We just had a chit chat and nothing talk about the business. I continue to maintain a good relationship with these people as I believe at the particular time that they will support me if I run my own business in future."

The relationship with customer staff is not only limited with the existing decision makers. It is also to develop a relationship with other staff that potentially will become a decision maker of the customer organisation in the future. These personal are mainly a junior management who are groomed to take over the management in future. A continuous relationship is crucial for business sustainability as far as the owner manager is concerned.

> "…most of my friends just talk with few important people in the customer organisation. They bring these people for drink and entertainment…hoping they will always get a priority in the business. However, they forgot that these people might leave the company or being replaced by somebody else in the future. That's why many of them lost the business when somebody becomes a new in-charge. For me. I'm OK to mingle around with anybody in the customer organisation and not restricted myself with the key person only. It is not cost me so much money and time to attract their attention… it could be only a few ringgit for a tea and some "kuih" during the break. But, these give advantages to me to start introduce myself particularly those are potential decision makers."

To distinguish their service, the owner manager in this organisation does not only consult the customer on their expertise, but he is willing to make some effort to assist the customer in other areas that are not in his scope.

> "you know…when customer treat you as their buddy… anything they will ask you to solve…. sometimes I feel like their PA (laugh). It is very hassle when the request is not within your expertise. But, I always think positive on this… we must help them only they will help us."

4.1.5 The findings on Case A

4.1.5.1 Finding on first research question

The profitability of the business is always a concern to the owner manager due to cash flow constraints. This is a common issue among SMEs as they do not allocate any budget for marketing. The spending for marketing activities is treated as operation spending as it is unstructured and ad hoc. The owner manager stated as follows:

> "We are not like big companies that have budget for advertising and promotion (A&P). What I spending mainly involve in maintaining the relationship with customer… just went out for tea, lunch or dinner only. Our margin is around 15%..... and if customer always ask entertainment...... 'I'm die…'.…The more money spent on marketing will further reduce the profit margin. Hence, we are not keen to spending much on marketing."

The owner manager also indicated that his personal lifestyle also sometimes hinders the speed of his marketing effort, as follows:

> "I can make friend with anybody in the business. However, I cannot entertain customer that always asking for 'drink or clubbing' as this not my personal lifestyle."

Personal competency plays a significant role in this process. The owner manager noted that his decisions relied heavily on past experience, and rated the impact of his own personal competency as "significant". The owner manager stated that:

> "I think my opinion has a big impact. It does not matter if other thinks that I am wrong… it is very

unlikely that I will follow. If I think that I should do it, then there is a pretty good chance of success."

When asked about how much of his personal competency was affected by personal knowledge, he responded:

"You have to be knowledgeable enough to understand the concepts, understand what actually happens and be able to ask questions. As well as that, I need to have enough confidence in my own ability to ask even dumb questions; only then I can find the answer."

Apart from that, the owner manager stressed that the ability to assess the risk is crucial for a small business. The owner manager quoted the following:

"Not all customers are good paymasters. There is a risk if we do not check customers' background carefully. We might end up running out of cash if we deal with them. Hence, it will be a waste to approach this kind of customers."

4.1.5.2 Finding on second research question

When asked about the decision method used in the decision process, the owner manager stated that no specific method was adopted in the decision process as he heavily relied on his previous experience. This is evident through following statement:

"As the owner of the company,... I involved in every single business decision of this company. Sincerely, I did not follow specific process in making the decision... and I don't care if other said I have made a wrong decision... what more concern is whether

I make a profit or not. But for sure, I will calculate how much the profit margin… it must at least 15%. This is a margin that I calculated some time back for my company to survive. I even share my costing to customer. To show my transparency to them… I think this is also part of marketing (laugh). Too transparent with customer also sometime not good… they keep renegotiating and pressing down our profit. But, I'll say sorry to them (customer) if the margin is less than 15%… How can I going to survive?"

The reason of the owner to use profit margin as a benchmark in the decision process mainly was motivate from his past experience. The owner manager was observed as a typical Chinese man who learned from his past working experience. This evident from the following statement:

"I don't know why big company had lot of meeting and paperwork. It always happens to me when I check status of my quotation. Their manger will always said management still discussing and analysing the cost. (Laugh)… big company always like that… complicated!

4.1.5.3 Finding on third research question

In this section, the research question was aimed at examining the source of information used by the owner manager in making marketing decision. Various sources of information were identified during the interview, which directly contributed to the decision process. As explained in previous section, the marketing practice for Company A was mainly restricted to the relationship marketing.

As such, customer is the main source of information as stated in following statement:

> "Insider information was really helpful… and can be considered as reliable. I know well some staff in procurement and finance whom to be my bowling partner. They sometime…. 'hint' me some useful information which can be used to against (laugh) their HOD. Without this information, sure their HOD simply will squeeze me…. particularly in costing."

However, other sources of information such as other owner manager, supplier, and lawyer were regarded as crucial by the owner manager to validate the information provided by the customer. The owner manager stated as follows:

> "However, I still need a referral from other source such as other owner manager, supplier or even a lawyer who had worked with the customer previously. These people can give a good feedback on how the customer behaves. It helps me to prepare a contingency plan to address any adverse possibility during the business transaction with a customer."

Information regarding decision was collected primarily by the owner manager from various resources. The information collected was then evaluated by the owner manager as indicative of the possible decision taken. An interesting finding in this case was that the owner manager also referred to his network in the bank to investigate the customer's financial capability. The owner manager stated as follows:

> "I will not simply accept the information provided by the customers. We can also do a cross check on

their financial situation when they start to revisit the cost structure due to their deteriorating profit. What I did was to contact my network in the banking sector that can validate the information provided by the customer."

4.1.5.4 Finding on fourth research question

In this section, the research question was aimed at investigating the influence of decision making method adopted by the decision maker to the decision outcome. As discussed earlier, the decision method adopted in this case was informal, which was considered by the owner manager to have fitted with their business requirement. The decision method used in this case, as claimed by the owner manager, increased customers' confidence due to the speed of the decision. The owner manager stated as follows:

> "As a decision maker, I can give immediate decision on customer inquiry and this actually makes them more confident and they trust us."

All decision phases were noted during the process. There were initial concerns as the decision had to be made quickly. This led to some uncertainty regarding the decision process. The owner manager considered that the decision had elements of subjectivity given the constraints imposed and urgency of the situation. However, the owner manager was happy with the outcome of the current process even though he faced difficulties in "getting sufficient information" to meet the process requirements. Apart for that, the owner manager recalled that the existing process has given him a more flexibility to manage the cash flow.

4.1.5.5 Summary

A summary of the process in relation to the marketing decision making model is depicted in Figure 4.2.

Figure 4.2: Summary of Case 1

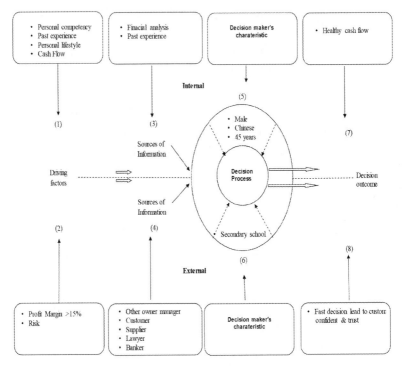

4.2 Case 2: Company B

4.2.1 Company background

Company B is a small-sized firm established in 2008. The internal environment within the organisation is a good evident from its high morale and dedicated staff. The organisation considers that the business environment in which it operates is highly competitive, and that customer requirements often drive the business. Organisation B involves in transportation and logistics service in Johor. The organisation currently provides services to a few major electronic companies in Johor.

4.2.2 Company structure

The company is jointly owned by two partners. However, only the owner manager designated as managing director actively involves in day-to-day management. The organisation is organised into two sections: transportation and freight forwarding. In transportation section, a supervisor is employed to manage 5 units of company trucks, while in freight forwarding section, two clerks handle customs clearance and shipping document. Operational decisions are generally led by the owner manager. However, for complex decisions that require high investment, the owner manager will consult with the partner to ensure that all risks are considered. Figure 4.3 illustrates organisation of Company B.

4.2.3 Interviewee

The interviewee was a 45-year old Malay entrepreneur. He graduated in Master of Logistics from the Universiti Teknologi Malaysia (UTM). Prior to owning the business, he worked with a public-listed company involving transport and logistics business for 20 years. He held various positions within the company especially in forwarding and shipping. The interview was conducted at the owner manager's office located at Johor Bahru.

Figure 4.3: Organisation chart of Company B

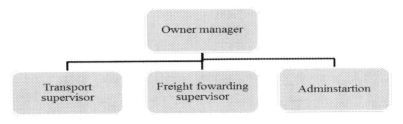

Source: Owner manager of Company B

4.2.4 Marketing practice in the company

The marketing practice in Company B started from a networking when the owner manager was still working with his previous company. During the period, he managed to establish strong networking with key personnel of customers, suppliers, and competitors. The owner manager state that:

> "I've been worked in this field for more than 20 years. In my previous company (haulage company), I used to liaise with them (existing customer) and support them wherever they face a difficulty. From time to time, they become close to me and trust me more than my previous company. When I move to other company, they are still following me and asking me to serve them from a new company."

Marketing practice in this company mainly focused on maintaining the existing relationship. It was not limited to customers, but also to suppliers and other business managers in the same sector. The size of company did not allow them to seize all the business opportunities. Some of business opportunities were a result of marketing activities done by other parties such as suppliers or other owner managers in the same industry. Hence, there was very little effort for a new or potential customer. The owner manager stressed the importance of good relationship.

> "It is not easy to penetrate a new business or market without knowing somebody in that company. Even in big company, relationship is important to penetrate the business. In our case, the business does not only come from our direct customer, but also from our networking that includes other owner manager and supplier."

The main activity in maintaining the relationship was through a social entertainment, which was different from the conventional marketing practice. No specific budget was allocated in marketing activity, but the owner manager would ensure there was no excessive spending. In this case, the owner manager stated that the quality of work or service would supersede other criteria in conventional marketing. Hence, it is crucial for the owner manager to ensure quality service to customer.

> "Basically, we are offering the same package as others. However, we are distinguished from them on what we can offer in terms of service quality."

There were challenges in the environment where the owner manager is currently operating. First is cost pressure from new comer. The owner manager stated as follows:

> "New comers tend to offer a very low rate in order to penetrate the business. Normally, we still can sustain due to our relationship with customers, but a continuous pressure could force us to revise the cost which further reduces the profit margin."

Secondly, penetrating a new business is always challenging due to relationship barrier. The owner manager stated as follows:

> "Sometimes we know their rate and we offer a more competitive rate. However, we still fail to get the business as the customer asks existing supplier to match the rate. This is because of the relationship. This scenario is a norm for SMEs environment."

During the interview, we also noticed that the given opportunity was a common practice in the business environment where the owner manager operated. In this practice, the business opportunity was also created from the suppliers and other owner managers in the same industry. The respondent stated as follows:

> "More than 50% of the business comes from our previous suppliers and other owner managers in the same industry."

4.2.5 The finding of case 2

4.2.5.1 Finding on first research question

The respondent believed personal competency based on past experience and education background had led him to become more inclusive, reassuring decision making process. The owner manager stated as follows:

> "I believe manager with better education and experience will have high competency in the business decision."

During the interview, we noticed that the education background of the owner manager heavily influenced his approach in business marketing. Knowledge in financial terms such as Cost Benefit

Analysis (CBA), Profit and Loss Analysis (P&L), and Return of Investment (ROI) evidently influenced his financial decision justification. The knowledge acquired from the MBA course had increased the owner manager's personal competency in making decision. The owner manager stated as follows:

> "I use Cost Business Analysis (CBA), ROI, and P&L methods to calculate the profitability of the business. These methods help to increase my confidence level to make a decision."

Apart from profit margin, payment term was also emphasised by the respondent. As a small company, cash flow was always a constraint in such business. Hence, fast collection was required for business survival. The owner manager emphasised that:

> "Cash flow is always our constraint. We don't want our money tied up for too long. An ideal payment term should be between 30 days to 45 days. Hence, I will not approach bad paymaster customer. It will make the company not sustainable."

During the meeting, the owner manager always emphasised on the importance to evaluate the feasibility of the business. This was evident in following statement:

> "We should be more cautious before making any decision. The risk of the business should properly be evaluated from different aspect as we might be misled by inaccurate information."

The size of the company and financial capability also influenced the decision process. This was evident in the following statement:

"We do not have much money for aggressive marketing. Our marketing practice is mainly based on current relationship. Furthermore, the size of company is unlikely to allow us to expand the business overnight."

Finally, the confidence built by the decision making process and the trust relationship formed the capstone factor to the decision, quoted as follows:

"…for long term, I must build up trust and confident with the customer that the relationship will benefit both parties."

4.2.5.2 Finding on second research question

During the interview, we noticed that two methods were used by the owner manager to handle different scenarios. Two main scenarios identified during the interview are as follows: 1) new business scenario; and 2) given opportunity scenario resulting from the relationship marketing.

i)   Given opportunity

Similar to case A, in given opportunity, the owner manager tended to use informal approach in the process of making marketing decision. This was evident through following statement:

"As mentioned earlier, my marketing approach was based on established relationship. Some of the businesses were a result from other marketing effort by my suppliers or other owner managers. They probably didn't have expertise or require support to manage the business. Accordingly, they offered me the business… Whenever I accept the offer, it is a part of continuous relationship."

In spite of informal approach claimed by the owner manager, we noticed an element of formal approach being applied parallel in the process. This was evident in the following statement:

> "Not every offer will be accepted immediately. In some of the case, I'll need time to do the evaluation and reference with other owner managers in the same industry for verification. But the most important thing is that I will calculate the feasibility of the business by employing financial indicators such as Cost Benefit Analysis (CBA), Profit and Loss Analysis (P&L), and Return of Investment (ROI)."

The emphasis on the financial analysis by the owner manager indicated the knowledge he gained from the formal education that could help him to make a better decision.

ii) New Business

In a new business scenario, the owner had established a guideline to approach the decision starting with market survey; financial analysis and evaluation of alternative were the main elements of the process. This was supported by following statement:

> "It is different for a new customer. Firstly, I'll do a market survey to collect information directly from the site. Then, I'll do financial analysis to calculate the feasibility of the business and consultation with other owner managers for their opinion and feedback. Lastly, I'll evaluate the options in hand to be offered to the customer."

4.2.5.3 Finding on third research question

The respondent collected a broad range of data that impacted on the decision. A wide set of information was used to perform the evaluation, which was a mix of different sources. The primary sources of information were knowledge gained from formal education and past working experience, which increased the owner manager personnel competency. The respondent described that:

> "Theory and practical knowledge from MBA course and past working experience made me more competent in handling day-to-day business requirements. The combination of these factors has equipped me to face current business challenges."

Other important source of information was information collected from customers, whom the owner manager felt crucial in the process. The owner manager stated as follows:

> "They are a big part of running the business and are really crucial to the outcome of the decision."

Other sources of information were other owner managers and suppliers who contributed significantly in the process. The other source of information reported during the meeting was a consultant. However, the owner manager had only used a consultant once who had costed him a great deal of money, and he received no useful assistance from the consultant. The owner manager had also referred to a lawyer for advice in legal aspect. A market survey was also carried out to enhance the quality of the decision. The respondent stated as follows:

> "I am not convinced if I did not personally observe the market. In one case, I sat for six hours

at the customs complex just to observe the truck movement."

4.2.5.4 Finding on fourth research question

The decision process was thorough and followed a generally well-understood approach within the company. The use of the financial analyses such as CBA, ROI, & P&L made the decision stronger, and "check and balance" was needed for such an important decision.

In this case, there were no delays or interrupts noted, possibly due to previous experience and the owner manager's competency in driving the data collection and analysis process prior to reaching decision. The customers' requirements were the overriding issue in respect of the process. In the case of Company B, the owner manager has been involved in this type of decision in recent years and has the process well-established and capable of being implemented quickly and efficiently. The owner manager added that his direct involvement in marketing decision will increase customer's confidence and trust as the decision can be made in a reasonable speed. This definitely would increase the value proposition in the relationship. The owner manager stated as follows:

> "In my experience with previous employer, approval was required from the superior for any proposal to customers and in certain cases the proposal was rejected after being discussed with the customers. As a result, customers have lost confidence and we lost the opportunity to get the business."

It is apparent that direct involvement of the owner manager in the decision process has led to desired outcome regardless the method adopted for the process.

4.2.5.5 Summary

A summary of the process in relation to the decision making model is depicted in Figure 4.4.

Figure 4.4: Summary of case 2

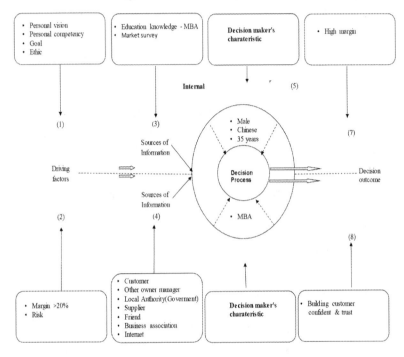

4.3 Case 3: Company C

4.3.1 Company background

Company C is a family-owned company founded in the early 1980's. This organisation has gone through various iterations before changing its name as used today in 2006. Organisation C involves in various trading businesses especially from China. The company also provides transportation service for cement industry in Johor.

4.3.2 Company structure

The organisation operation is headed by a general manager who is assisted by particular operational functions within the company. All of these operational staff have extensive transport industry experience and a range of tertiary qualifications from degrees in commerce, logistics, and economics to graduate qualifications in business administration and management. The organisation chart as advised by the respondent is illustrated in Figure 4.5.

Figure 4.5: Organisation chart of Company C

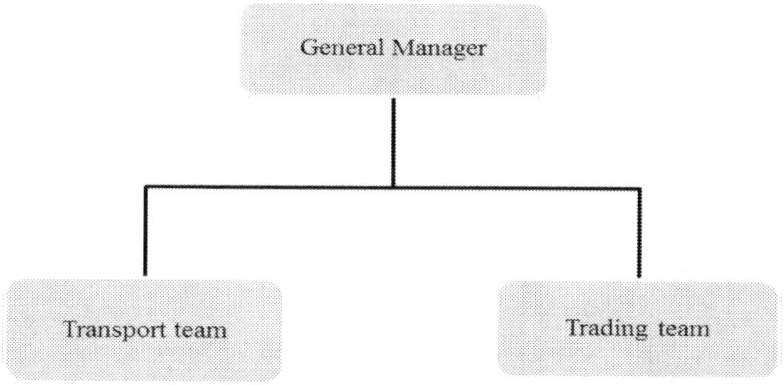

Source: General Manager, Company C

4.3.3 Interviewee

The respondent is a 29-year old Chinese entrepreneur. He is a graduate in Master of Business and Management (MBA). In 2005, he joined his father's company and later took over the management as a General Manager.

4.3.4 Marketing practice in the company

The marketing practice in this organisation is led by the respondent, whom is also the General Manager of the company. During the interview, we noticed that different approaches were used separately for trading and transport business. The interviewee stated as follows:

> "When I took over the management from my father, I start to venture a trading business which I think is very prospective to support the current transport business. I have a share partner whom to be my classmate during my MBA study. Both of us jointly manage this business which concentrates to explore business opportunities in China which totally different 'games' from the transport business."

In transport business, the approach was based on establishing networking where the word of mouth effect played an important role to spread out their service into the market. The owner manager stated as follows:

> "Some of our customers recommended us to their friends and this automatically helps to promote our service... and some of them had dealt with us in the past. My father has put much effort to introduce our company in the market... and his good character especially in mingle with people make him well accepted in the market... I think."

The situation was similar for trading business where networking was still a focal point to penetrate the market. However, the approach was slightly different due to the difference in business culture. In China, a local influencer, which is normally a government officer, is required to promote the business. The owner manager stated as follows:

> "We have to understand the market before we invest especially when dealing with people from China.

We have to meet many local authorities to establish the relationship. Fortunately, one of my uncles is working as a government officer there and this helps a lot."

4.3.5   The Finding of Case 3

4.3.5.1 Finding on first research question

There was prominent evidence that the personal competency, which was built from the education background of the respondent, drove the process of decision making. This was evident through the application of financial tools as stated in following statement:

> "The profit earned from the business should be equivalent with the effort. Hence, I set a minimum target of 20% in profit. This benchmark is reasonable for this industry due to high fluctuate in cost. I would not pursue the business if the margin below the target. I convince to use financial tool that I learned during my study to see the profitability of the business that I intend to peruse. I see many of my friend closes down the business due to underestimate of the cost… and some of them were in the same MBA class. It is funny!

It was important to calculate the profitability of the business during the marketing decision process to ensure the feasibility of the business and to eliminate one of the risks before pursuing with the business. This was evident in following quote:

> "Without proper evaluation, we might be exposed to the risk of not making money. I think this is a basic fundamental that many businessmen take

lightly due to lack understanding of financial tools. Some people may think that they are making an excessive profit without knowing that lot of cost is not included which effect their profit in the end."

Apart from financial return, the owner manager's personal vision, goal, and ethics also influenced the process of decision making. This was evident in the following statement:

"I have a vision to diversify my business and China is one of the good places to start as we face fierce competition locally especially in transport industry. There many transporters in the market chasing for the same 'cake'... and this pressing further the transport rate. But, when I start importing from China... I can further utilise my transportation division to involve in distributing of the product. The impact has never been thought before!! I believe many transporters will involve in trading business soon... especially when they see what I'm doing... and I am very positive on this as long as they are stay competitive without compromise the business ethics."

4.3.5.2 Finding of second research question

As a small organisation, informal and flexible approach is always preferred by the owner manager to be adopted in his business decision process. However, wide exposure and knowledge gained from formal education such as MBA might influence the way of the process being implemented. In this case, the elements of formal approach such as market survey, financial analysis, sourcing the information, and evaluation of option were raised during the interview. The respondent stated as follows:

"...it is difficult to answer (laugh). (Silent a while) Sincerely, I don't see myself as a critical person when making a decision.... and I prefer a simple and fast decision as this what customer want actually. But, without proper evaluation, we might fail to get the business our run at the loss. This is what I'm trying to balance in my decision. Probably, what I studied in MBA give me some insight in proper business methodology... such as make use of financial tools, market survey and accessing risk. (Laugh)... of course I'm not follow exactly like in the book, but it give different perception when making the decision. No doubt... MBA course gives me a different insight of marketing perspective. Except for transport business that is traditionally based on word of mouth effect, a more structured approach is used in trading."

4.3.5.3 Finding on third research question

The discussion on source of information for case C will be split in two scenarios.

i) Transport Business

Mixed sources of information were quoted by the respondent in the process, which included customer, other owner managers, suppliers, and social friends, as in the following quote:

"Everything surround us are the information... it is depend on how we want to use it. In transport industry, a networking is extremely important and can be consider as fast and reliable source of information. The information within the networking circle includes our friend that working at customer organisation, our business friend whom also has similar business, supplier and our friends."

Information supplied by customers' key personal was regarded as an important information source in this segment. The respondent stated that he relied heavily on customers' documents such as rate, sales forecast, and budget. In this regard, the respondent stated as follows:

> "The best strategy to seize the customer (smile)... is to have insider informants. It would much easier if we know well the decision maker.... This is common tactic in any business to develop relationship with the customer decision maker. For my case, I'm might lucky as some of them are my school mate or I have known them before they are promoting to be a decision maker. For me... having a good relationship with customer decision maker is ticket for us to access crucial information such as rate, sale forecast, budget, and etc.... which is essential for the evaluation."

As this business segment was inherited from his family, the owner manager would also make a reference to his father before making any final decision. The respondent stated as follows:

> "My father knows most of the customers and could advise me which customers I should approach. He has been in this industry in so many years... which of course he has a good networking in the market. I regard him as my inspiration and my most important source of information."

ii) Trading Business

In general, information in this segment was obtained from market survey, other owner managers, suppliers, and local authorities. The information apparently played a crucial role in the process to reach the decision. The owner manager stressed the important of this source in the following quote:

> "Dealing with Chinese in mainland is not easy as most of them are cunning... even myself a Chinese... don't trust them. All their word must be validated and documented. If not, they will find a way to cheat you. We had to come all the way from Malaysia just to meet up with supplier and make a market survey to validate the market potential. There are many cases reported that the syndicate claimed as a supplier approaching Malaysia businessman and promise a return from the business which is not exit. To deal with this, we have to use Chinese local authority to involve in our business discussion. It is apparently that the Chinese are bit worried if we know somebody in local their authority. I heard that punishment for cheating offence is very heavy in China... so they are bit worried on that. Luckily, one of my uncle is working there as a local authority. He helps me to identify a genuine supplier as he had a good contact among the local business man. ...and because of this, I never being cheated so far."

The information technology such as the Internet was utilised by the owner manager to search for information pertaining to the business. The respondent stated as follows:

> "As said earlier… we must be extra careful when dealing with Chinese. I really advise to those who want to deal with Chinese guy to verify their company in details. One of the platforms we can use is to check in the Internet. There is community in the Internet that actively reported the scam case by revealing the name of the people or organisation. So, whenever I received a business card from new supplier or prospect buyer… the first thing I do is to check if there any discussion on that person or particular company. We can easily find out if the businessman had a bad record in the past."

Apart from financial return, the owner manager's personal vision, goal, and ethics also influenced the process of decision making. This was evident in the following statement:

> "I have a vision to expand my business and China is one of the good places to start as we face fierce competition locally. However, I'll not compromise business ethics during the process."

4.3.5.4 Finding on fourth research question

The decision processes led by the owner manager was regarded as a success, considering the flexibility of the approach adopted in different markets. The positive decision outcomes from the process can be primarily attributed to the building of trust by the customers. The use of the financial analyses such as CBA, ROI, and P&L gave the decision the prominence and "checks and balances" needed for such an important decision.

"As a small organisation, we are expected to feedback faster to customer in decision process due to less bureaucracy. I think I had successfully blend this aspect together with my knowledge during the process of making the decision which translate in customer trust and at the same time make sure the profitability of the business."

4.3.5.5 Summary

A summary of the process in relation to the decision making model is depicted in Figure 4.6.

Figure 4.6: Summary of case 3

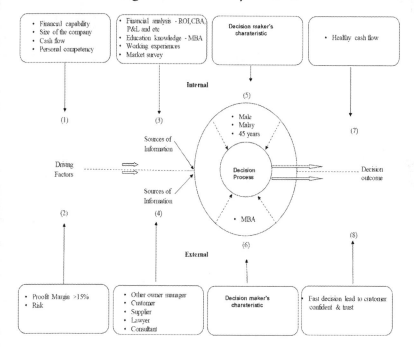

4.4   Case 4: Company D

4.4.1   Company background

This family-owned company was started in 1979 and have nearly 30 years of experience in transportation business. It was started by the owner manager's late father with one truck partnering with his brother. Presently, the company owns 20 tankers. It originally started with transporting palm oil, and is currently expanding to other product.

4.4.2   Company structure

The company structure is very much family-based similar to pyramid style where the father is the leader to look after the entire company. He is assisted by 3 sons who are the managers in different areas such as marketing, procurement, and operation. When the father passed away in 2009, there was no leader in the company and the organisation structure has no leader as all the sons were equally responsible to the company. This created duplicated works among the siblings, and there was no direction in the company. Concerning the future of the company, all the siblings agreed to restructure the organisation to avoid duplicated works among them. As a result, the organisation structure was driven by three main functions, which were operation, business development and marketing, and procurement. A leader was elected among the siblings to lead the company. The organisation chart based on the information gathered from the respondent is illustrated in Figure 4.7.

Figure 4.7: Organisation chart of Company D

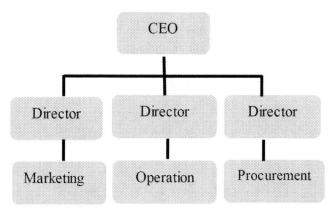

Source: CEO, Organisation D

4.4.3 Interviewee

The interview was conducted at respondent's office at Rawang, Selangor. The interview was regarding the respondent's intention to expand the business to east Malaysia. The interviewee is the director of the company who is in charge of business development and marketing. He is a graduate of Harvard University in marketing, and has served for the company for the past 10 years. As family organisation, he jointly manages the company with the other two siblings. The interviewee is an IT savvy and has heavily invested in information technology infrastructure especially related to trucking.

4.4.4 Marketing practice in the company

The company started as a family business where the traditional hearsay and word of mouth approaches were widely used. The marketing activities were led by the owner's late father whom used to spending much time on meeting customers who required their tanker service. During his tenure, the owner had never spent a single cent of money on advertising and promotion (A&P). He was quiet reluctant to spend on advertising and promotion due to lack of exposure and confidence. In 2008, the responsibility of marketing was taken over by the youngest son whom graduated from Harvard University. The son managed to convince the owner (father) to change the business approach and they started to spend on A&P. At the beginning, they spent RM2,000 to place a small advertising in the STAR newspaper for the water tanker service. They managed to secure 3 water tankers to supply water in Selangor & Johor during the water crisis in 2008. From that point, the respondent managed to convince the family to use A&P in their marketing activities. Presently, they are spending around 10% of the revenue for A&P, which include trade magazine, newspaper, website, and newsletter. These are the A&P areas used to market their services. Even though they have been established for 30 years, still many people do not know about their service. Every month they will place advertisement in any one of the trade magazines to update the latest move by the company. Other than that, they also do a direct mail to 460 palm oil mills in Peninsular Malaysia to remind them about their services. The sales increased to 40% when they started using A&P.

4.4.5 The finding of case 4

4.4.5.1 Finding on first research question

In this case, limited formal documentation was produced to justify the decision. Justifications were primarily stated through emails among the directors. As noted previously, a formal business case was never developed. The primary justification provided was to increase the market size.

There were two main driving factors cited for the decision, which did not appear in any communication or documentation of the time, but were discussed by the interviewee. The first was concerning the margin earned from the business. It was calculated that the margin for this area was 15% higher than the Peninsular Malaysia.

"The main decision maker is margin. Other is manageable. Margin is driven with the increase of cost. In *Semenanjung* (Peninsular Malaysia), we go for 10–15%. In Sabah, 30% because of different cost structure. This is very lucrative for transport business."

The second driving factor was concerning the established relationship with a few millers. The respondent explained that the relationship with a few millers in Sabah also contributed to the decision. The respondent explained as follows:

"A big part of it initially was the relationship... one of the biggest things... you need to get a feel whether you're going to be there with these guys... certainly cost is a major factor but this factor is also equally important... the fact is that they are inviting us."

The confidence built by financial return and the relationship formed the capstone factor to the decision. Of the factors examined above, the respondent rated the contribution margin as the most important factor. The respondent explained as follows:

"A main concern is the rate or margin. Based on my calculation, we require 20–25% margin to survive. However, I noticed, the transporter over there is enjoying 30% margin, which is superb. Margin is very high there."

However, the respondent also expressed his concern on possible risk that might hamper his planning as stated in the following quote:

"We have to be careful when introducing our service to this market. Some competitors may not be contented and try to stop our presence in this area. Of course we don't want this to happen... it will not benefit to everybody. Instead of introducing our own fleet there, we are partnership them as our subcontractor... this will make them feel more secure and reduce the cautious. However, not all transporters are willing to work with us... and this still a threat to us."

Apart of the above mentioned factors, the influence of personal vision also clearly mentioned in this interview as following quote:

"...No doubt that we are quite established in Peninsular Malaysia... but if we want to growing, we have to go some else... which I think Sabah is a good start."

4.4.5.2 Finding on second research question

It was clear that knowledge earned by the respondent from his tertiary education distinguished the approach taken in making marketing decision making as compared to other SMEs in this study. In this instance, a procedure in making marketing-related decision has been established in this organisation. The respondent stated as follows:

"After consulting with MPOB... I took flight to Sabah to visit few millers that have similar operation in Peninsular Malaysia. This miller used to be our loyal customer in Peninsular Malaysia for some many years. Some of the decision maker knew me well while they are working at Peninsula Malaysia. It is quiet easy to get their cooperation especially to collect the data pertaining to volume, transport rate and etc... They also introducing me with few transporter that potentially can be our subcontractor. After that, I contacted directly the transporter and discuss on the possibility to partnership in this project. From the discussion with the transporter, I manage to collect some crucial operation information that later to be used in the evaluation. All these information will be analysed to determine the profitability of the business and for other director approval. This is essential to prevent us from being misleading. As such, a procedure has been established."

4.4.5.3 Finding on third research question

This section examines the source of information used by the respondent. Obtaining relevant information was found to be vital phase in the marketing decision making process. The respondent, as the director of the company, began to collect the information about the target market in order to access the prospective of potential new market. The information was obtained mainly through various sources such Malaysia Palm Oil Board (MPOB), Millers and Transporters, and searching in the Internet and trade magazines. In addition, the respondent had extensive knowledge in this area, which was gained through a networking with the MPOB.

The owner manager relied strongly on trade media especially MPOB production figure. Every month, MPOB will publish production figure for the next 2–3 years. This information was used by the respondent as a guideline for forecasting on the tanker demand in Peninsular Malaysia. The owner manager stated as follows:

"This information is very useful. I can always forecast whether this particular year requires more attention and planning. It is because 90% of our sales come out from palm oil business."

The owner manager also relied on the miller to give the information particularly in relation to transport rate. The respondent stated as follows:

"We have friend in certain mill whom we will call to find ask for information. The information from these informants is crucial for negotiating with other transporter."

The owner manager also referred to other transporter for information gathering. He adopted a philosophy that competitor is irrelevant. He differentiated himself from others by heavily investing in information technology. The owner manager stated as follows:

"We have same equipment, same transport rule and human to drive. I make competition irrelevant through the technology."

4.4.5.4 Finding on fourth research question

The decision making process started with a market survey to help the owner manager indicate the feasibility of the business and drive more information to facilitate the process. The quality of information was regarded as sufficient to the owner manager to have a selection of options to make the decision. The owner manager stated as follows:

"I am satisfied with the process and the quality of information collected from various sources. It is regarded as a success and I keep reviewing it for improvement."

4.4.5.5 Summary

A summary of the process in relation to the decision making model is depicted in Figure 4.8.

Figure 4.8: Summary of case 4

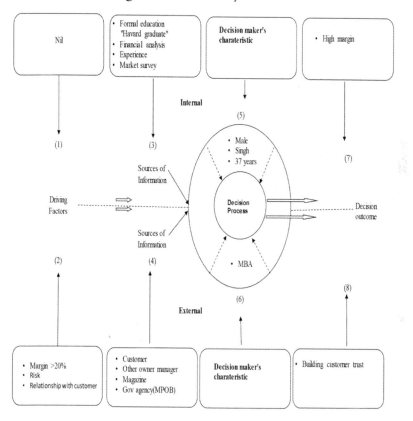

4.5   Cross Case Finding about Research Issues

This section presents the cross case analysis of the data collected using the methodology described in Chapter Three. The aim of the section is to address the research questions through the results of this analysis. The section begins by summarising and contrasting the findings of the four case studies examined in this research. This is followed by a comparative literature review of findings.

Data gathering occurred sequentially in four organisations, and was halted when theoretical saturation was reached. As noted by Auerbach (2005), theoretical saturation is part of the sampling process, and forms a mechanism to signal when an appropriate amount of data has been collected. This method is supported by Sekaran (2003).

4.5.1   Finding on first research question

Three types of decision making methods were indicated by the decision makers from the qualitative survey. The decision methods were identified as formal, informal, and combination of formal and informal. Three decision makers from Company A, B, and C used informal method in the process of making marketing decision. The adoption of this method was mainly motivated through establishment of marketing relationship. This typical approach has been described by Gilmore et al. (2001) and Woods and Joyce (2003). Out of these three companies, only Company A was deemed to be informal. This was evident in the following quote:

> "I always refer to previous experience as a guide for improvement."
> [Company A]

However, there was an evidence to suggest that the process was more structured than indicated by the decision makers although informal decision making processes were present in these organisations. The influence of formal method is evident in the following quotes:

> "...I will calculate the feasibility of the business by employing financial indicators such as Cost Benefit Analysis (CBA), Profit and Loss Analysis (P&L), and Return of Investment (ROI)."
> [Company B]

> "MBA course gives me a different insight of marketing perspective. Except for transport business that is traditionally based on word of mouth effect, a more structured approach is used in trading."
> [Company C].

Meanwhile, it was reported that Company D adopted structured approach assessment to gather a feedback from the market. This feedback was then used as a part of the decision making procedure established in this organisation. The respondent stated as follows:

> "It is essential to have a procedure to prevent us from being misleading. As such, a procedure has been established."
> [Company D]

There was similarity among the decision makers in Company B, C, and D as all of them were MBA graduates. This perhaps may explain the reason they were willing to adopt structured or formal approach in marketing decision process. As suggested by Wasilezuk (2000), the education level received by the decision maker may influence the adoption of decision method in the process.

4.5.2 Finding on second research question

In order to understand how decisions were made, data related to the specific information used by the decision makers were collected. 15 sources of information were indicated by the decision makers. These sources were past experience, formal education, other business managers, friends, suppliers, customers, the Internet, external private consultants, SMEs associations, government agencies, family, media, bank, seminar, and trade exhibition.

Majority of the respondents indicated that past experience, other business managers, and customers were the three most important sources of information. This finding apparently challenges the previous study by Elaine *et al.* (2007) that suggests customers, suppliers, and other owner managers as the three most important sources of information for SMEs. The emergence of past experience in this study supports the argument that SMEs have gained relevant advantages from previous work experience (Marc, 2001), which has built up their competitive advantages in decision making process.

The next important source of information was formal education, which was indicated by decision makers from Company B, C, and D. The importance of this source to the decision makers was expected as all of them had attended MBA course prior to setting up the business. The knowledge gained from MBA course may change the way a decision maker approaches the problem or issue to reach to a decision.

The other important sources of information were friends/ social networks, suppliers, family, Internet, SMEs associations, and government. The importance of networking components to provide the information for SME decision is getting less important as the decision makers' competency increased through their working experience and education. Furthermore, the increase in IT awareness among the owner managers has encouraged them to search for alternative sources, with Internet has emerged as a new source of information. The least used sources of information indicated by the decision makers were media, bank, seminar, and trade exhibition.

Hairul Rizad and Abu Bakar

This finding was expected, as suggested by Elaine (2007). However, unexpectedly, trade exhibition was also the least used source of information by the decision makers even though the Government through its agencies such as SME Corp and MITI has constantly organised the exhibition to promote SMEs. This finding perhaps demonstrates the differences between the small group and the whole industry, which will further be examined in the comparison between qualitative and quantitative results.

4.5.3   Finding on third research question

Thirteen driving forces were identified to influence the decision makers in making marketing decision process.

Four driving factors were indicated by the decision makers as the most influential in marketing decision process. These driving factors are personal competency, personal experience, financial return, and risk size. The decision makers' personal competency and personal experience were described by Man (2001) as significantly linked to the decision making performance, and mainly determined by working experience and tertiary education level (Barnes & Winterton, 2001). This perhaps supports the reason for the SME decision makers indicating past experience and education level as the two most important sources of information in marketing decision process. The importance of financial return and risk size to the SMEs business decision process has been discussed extensively by Joensuu *et al.* (2009). Financial return and risk size are common indicators and motivators for decision makers in any type of organisation to pursue their businesses.

The second most important driving factors indicated by majority of the decision makers were long-term business relationship and company financial capability. Maintaining long-term relationship is crucial for SMEs to ensure the sustainability of the business due to limitation in size to compete with large the organisations (Simpson *et al.*, 2006). Restricted financial capability is a common characteristic of SME businesses (Salleh *et al.*, 2006). However, it was argued that SMEs often misunderstood the concept of marketing, and they did not even realise that they have used it in their business. It is also understood that SMEs did not allocate any budget for marketing expenses; they rather recognised it as operating expenses (Dwyer *et al.*, 2009).

Next, the third most important driving factors were personal vision, market size, and size of the company. The low importance of personal vision among SME decision makers indicates that SMEs in general are still bound with the silo mentality due to company characteristics. This finding also supports the argument that SMEs in Malaysia prefer to "stay small" in business (Hazlian & Shen, 2009) due to lack of vision among the decision makers to foresee the benefit and potential of effective marketing process (Oviatt & McDougal, 2005). The influence of market size and size of the company does not play a crucial role in marketing decision due to the nature of SMEs marketing characteristics that only deal with a few customers (McCartan-Quinn & Carson, 2003) that they felt comfortable.

The findings on personal lifestyle, business association, and ethical and social consideration were the least quoted factors by the respondents. But, these probably did not represent the whole industry. This will be further examined in quantitative survey.

4.5.4 Finding on fourth research question

Majority of the decision makers perceived that they were "very satisfied" with the result of decision outcome. This indicated that the adoption of decision method was appropriate for their decision process. This was evident through following quotes:

> "As a decision maker, I can give immediate decision on customer inquiry and this actually makes them more confident and they trust us."
> [Company A]

"In my experience with previous employer, approval was required from the superior for any proposal to customers and in certain cases the proposal was rejected after being discussed with the customers. As a result, customers have lost confidence and we lost the opportunity to get the business."
[Company B]

"I am satisfied with the process and the quality of information collected from various sources. It is regarded as a success and I keep reviewing it for improvement."
[Company C]

4.5.5 Summary of cases

Table 4.1: Summary of Case A, B, C, and D

Case	Driving factor	Decision method	Source of information	Decision Outcome
A	Personal competency Personal lifestyle Personal experience Profit margin (financial return) Cash Flow Risk size	Informal	Past experience Other business managers Friends/social networks Customers External private sector consultants Banks or other financial institutions	Satisfied

Case	Driving factor	Decision method	Source of information	Decision Outcome
B	Personal competency Profit margin (financial return) Cash flow Company financial capability Size of company Risk size	Informal/ Formal	Past experience Formal education Other business managers Suppliers Customers External private sector consultants Banks or other financial institutions	Satisfied
C	Personal vision Personal competency Goal setting Ethical and social consideration Personal experience Profit margin (financial return) Company financial capability Risk size	Informal/ Formal	Past experience Formal education Other business managers Friends/social networks Suppliers Customers Family Internet SMEs associations Government (SME Corp., Matrade, etc.)	Satisfied

Hairul Rizad and Abu Bakar

Case	Driving factor	Decision method	Source of information	Decision Outcome
D	Personal vision	Formal	Past experience	Satisfied
	Personal competency		Formal education	
	Long term business relationship		Other business managers	
			Customers	
	Personal experience		Family	
	Profit margin (financial return)		Media (including TV, newspapers, etc.)	
	Market size		Internet	
	Risk size		Seminars	
			Trade exhibition	
			SMEs associations	
			Government (SME Corp., Matrade, etc.)	

4.6   Summary

This chapter provides cross case results through outlining the similarities and differences among the four cases in relation to the research questions. Accordingly, based on the cross case findings, the survey instrument for quantitative survey was developed.

CHAPTER 5

QUANTITATIVE ANALYSIS

5.0 Introduction

This chapter is dedicated to addressing the issue of analysis and interpretation of data collected from the survey instrument, i.e., questionnaire. In this research, Statistical Package for Social Sciences (SPSS) was used for data analysis. In this chapter, data are presented according to research question (RQ). Both descriptive and inferential statistics are used in the data presentation. This chapter ends with a summary of the key issues discussed. Figure 5.1 outlines the key section of this chapter.

Figure 5.1: Chapter Five Organisational Flow

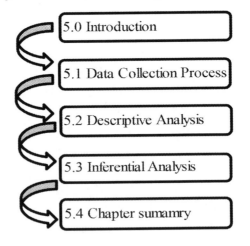

5.0 Introduction

5.1 Data Collection Process

5.2 Descriptive Analysis

5.3 Inferential Analysis

5.4 Chapter sumamry

5.1 Data Collection Process

In this research, the survey questionnaire was sent out through email to SMEs firm directed towards SMEs owners or someone whom they considered to be a qualified person to complete the questionnaire. Follow-ups through phone call and email to nonresponders were conducted. Organisations participating in the study were selected randomly from the SMEs list provided by SME Corp. The random selection allowed for the inclusion of a variety of companies across a number of different industries. Of the 500 firms contacted, only 182 completed the survey, resulting in a response rate of 36%. This rate was regarded as sufficient to move to the next stage of evaluating the data. According to Aeker *et al.* (2004), data received from field survey should undergo some preparatory procedures by translating the data collected into a form that is appropriate for a data analysis. This process suggests examining the raw data for omissions, accuracy, legibility, and consistency, in addition to dealing with issues of missing responses as well as nonresponse error (Aeker *et al.*, 2004). Therefore, in this research, Microsoft Excel software was used at the first stage to identify coding error. Then, the data were imported to SPSS for further verification, and frequencies were used to identify any coding error.

5.2 Descriptive Analysis

This section discusses descriptive statistics of the data focusing on certain key issues related to respondents' profile, business profile, and findings on research question.

5.2.1 Respondents' profile

The respondents' characteristics were categorised into six groups, namely ethnic, gender, and age, level of education, position held, and years in present position. Table 5.1 presents the respondents' profile.

A total of 182 respondents participated in this study. The largest group of respondents identified themselves as Malay (57.1%), followed by Chinese (28.6%) and Indian (14.3%).

Majority of the respondents indicated that they were male (85.7%), while the remaining 14.3% were female respondents.

With respect to age, the ages below 40 years old accounted for 50% of the sample population, indicating high number of young entrepreneurs in this study. The remaining 50% of the sample were between 40 and 55 years old. This demographic finding was important for this study as majority of the respondents can be considered still in their prime of life, thus making them more willing to share their opinions and experiences on issues under investigation.

Next, majority of the respondents indicated that they took formal education beyond high school, with 64% stating that they had a university degree, followed by 14.3% who received Master's degree or higher, while only 14.3% of the respondents had completed only up to high school or lower levels of education. This finding indicates the importance of tertiary education to business owners in managing their business.

The survey was initially targeted to SMEs owner managers in order to ensure that the respondents were in a position exercising authority or influence over the marketing decisions. If the owners were not active in decision making or felt that someone else in the firm was better to respond to the survey questions, then this person was considered acceptable. Majority of the respondents of the survey were owners (managing director, 50%; CEO, 7.1%) followed by general manager (21.43%), senior manager (7.1%), and other positions (14.32%). The significant involvements of decision makers in this study would be beneficial as they were considered to be highly versed with the issues under investigation.

Table 5.1: Respondents' profile

n=182

Item	Frequency	Percentage (%)
Ethnicity		
Malay	104	57.1
Chinese	52	28.6
Indian	26	14.3
Gender		
Male	156	85.7
Female	26	14.3
Age		
Less than 40 years old	91	50
Between 40 and 55 years old	91	50
Level of education		
High school	26	14.3
Diploma	39	21.4
Bachelor's degree	91	50
Master's degree	26	14.3
Designated position		
Managing Director	91	50
Chef Executive Office	13	7.1
General Manager	39	21.4
Senior Manager	13	7.1
Others	26	14.3
Length of time working in designated position		
Less than 1 year	26	14.3
Between 1–3 years	26	14.3
Between 3–4 years	52	28.6
More than 5 years	78	42.9

The majority of respondents stated that they had served less than 5 years in their current position (57.2%), while 42.9% of those surveyed indicated that they had been with the company for more than 5 years.

From these results, two conclusions can be made. Firstly, the results support that tertiary education is important to most SMEs business owners, and they have necessary working experience prior to setting up the business. Secondly, the results also imply that, for most of the respondents, business is not their first career choice.

5.2.2 Business profile

The focus of this section is to examine the business' profile in which the respondents served. Four distinctive particulars were targeted, including business activity, annual sales turnover, number of employees, and business stages, as illustrated in Table 5.2.

Two categories of SMEs namely Building & Construction and Transport (28.6%) shared the same percentage, and both were the largest business activities of this study. They were followed by Manufacturing and Trading (14.3%) and Electronic & Automotive by (7%). These various business activities surveyed were to keep with the goal of the study, i.e., to survey SMEs from a variety of business categories that represented the population of SMEs in Malaysia.

As noted in Chapter Two, one of the criteria to define the size of the company based on the National SME Development Council (2005) guideline was the annual sales turnover. As indicated in Table 5.2, more than 86% of the respondents earned more than RM250,000 a year. Based on this result, we can conclude that the majority of the respondents in this study were in the category of small and medium-sized enterprises.

Table 5.2: Respondents' business profile

n=182

Item	Frequency	Percentage (%)
Business activity		
Automotive	13	7.1
Building & Construction	52	28.6
Electric & Electronics	13	7.1
Manufacturing	26	14.3
Trading	26	14.3
Transport	52	28.6
Annual sales turnover		
Less than RM250 K	26	14.3
RM250 K–RM1 mil	39	21.4
RM1 mil–RM5 mil	65	35.7
RM5 mil–RM10 mil	13	7.1
More than 10 mil	39	21.4
Number of employees		
Less than 5	13	7.1
From 5 to 20	78	42.9
From 21 to 50	39	21.4
From 51 to 100	13	7.1
More than 100	39	21.4
Business stage		
Early growth	91	50
Later growth	39	21.4
Stability	52	28.6

More than 80% of the respondents employed more than 5 workers in their business, and only 7% had less than 5 workers. This finding supports the finding on annual sales turnover, i.e., most of the companies were in the category of small and medium-sized enterprises.

In terms of business growth, 50% of the respondents indicated that they were in the early growth of the business development. Next, 21% of the respondents described themselves as being in the later growth stage, while the remaining 29% of the respondents described their businesses as in stability.

The demographic results from the survey indicate that majority of the SMEs were small and medium-sized enterprises with fewer than 20 employees although the range of annual sales for these firms was spread out over several categories. Most firms were considered in early businesses growth as they had been in operation for less than 10 years, and surveyed respondents were most likely to be educated owners or managers who have considerable experience working with their company. The demographics of the survey were reflective of the demographics of the Malaysian environment.

5.2.3 Decision making process

In order to gain an understanding about the process in making marketing decision, respondents were asked to indicate their personal opinion in the following aspects: decision method, source of information, driving factor, and decision outcome.

5.2.4 Driving factors (Q1)

In this question, the respondents were asked to identify the factors influencing their decision making, as shown in Table 5.3.

71.4% of the respondents (35.7%, to large extent; 35.7%, to very large extent) indicated that personal vision was important in driving the process, while 25.3% of the respondents selected to some extent and the remaining (7.1%) selected to small extent.

Next, personal competency was also regarded as important in this survey where 71.4% of the respondents (56.6%, to large extent; 14.8%, to very large extend) indicated the importance of this factor in the marketing decision process. 21.4% of the respondents indicated that to some extent they had been able to use their personal competency in making marketing decision, while the remaining selected to small extent (7.1%).

Table 5.3: Driving factors

Driving factor	Not at all	To small extent	To some extent	To large extent	To very large extent	Mean	Std. Dev.
Personal vision		13 (7.1%)	46 (25.3%)	65 (35.7%)	58 (35.7%)	3.92	0.92516
Personal competency		13 (7.1%)	39 (21.4%)	103 (56.6%)	27 (14.8%)	3.79	0.7798
Long-term business relationship		19 (10.4%)	39 (21.4%)	72 (39.6%)	52 (28.6%)	3.86	0.9506
Goal setting			65 (35.7%)	52 (28.67%)	65 (35.7%)	4.00	0.8474
Personal and lifestyle consideration	23 (12.6%)	23 (12.6%)	49 (26.9%)	59 (32.4%)	28 (15.4%)	3.252	1.2312
Ethical and social consideration		16 (8.8%)	38 (20.9%)	96 (52.7%)	32 (17.6%)	3.79	0.83456
Personal experience		1 (0.5%)	49 (26.9%)	93 (51.1%)	39 (21.4%)	3.93	0.7098
Financial return		1 (0.5%)	26 (14.3%)	92 (50.5%)	63 (34.6%)	4.19	0.6903
Company financial capability			52 (28.6%)	91 (50%)	39 (21.4%)	3.93	0.7054
Market size		26 (14.3%)	65 (35.7%)	65 (35.7%)	26 (14.3%)	3.50	0.9088
Risk size	13 (7.1%)	13 (7.1%)	39 (21.4%)	78 (42.9%)	39 (21.4%)	3.64	1.1119
Size of company			91 (50%)	65 (35.7%)	26 (14.3%)	3.64	0.7198

Moreover, long-term business relationship was viewed as important by 68.2% of the respondents (39.6%, to large extent; 28.6%, to very large extent), while 21.4% of the respondents indicated to some extent and the remaining selected to small extent (10.4%).

Other than that, goal setting factor was viewed by 64.3% of the respondents as important in the process of decision making, while 35.7% of the respondents selected the option "to some extent".

The influence of personal lifestyle was viewed by most of the respondents (12.6%, not all; 12.6%, to small extent; 26.9%, to some extent) as an unimportant driving factor. Only 47.8% of the respondents indicated the option as an important driving factor.

Moreover, more than half of the respondents (52.79%, to large extent; 17.64%, to very large extent) indicated the importance of ethical and social consideration in the process of making marketing decision. The remaining 35.7% of the respondents indicated the scale "to small extent" (8.8%) and "to some extent" (20.9%), thus signifying the importance of this factor in driving the process of making marketing decision.

Other than that, the importance of personal experience in driving the process of making marketing decision was acknowledged by 72.5% of the respondents (51.1%, to large extent; 21.4%, to very large extent), while the remaining respondents (26.9%) selected the scale "to some extent" and (0.5%) selected the scale "to small extent".

Next, the most important factor revealed in this survey was financial return where majority of the respondent (85.1%) indicated the importance of this factor (50.5%, to large extent; 34.6%, to very large extent) in driving their marketing decision making. Only 14.3% of the respondents indicated that this factor only contributed to some extent in marketing decision making process.

Besides that, company financial capability was also perceived important by 71.4% of the respondents (50%, to large extent; 21.4%, to very large extent), while the remaining (28.6%) indicated less importance of this factor in marketing decision making process.

Next, half of the respondents (50%) perceived the importance of market size during decision process (35.7%, to large extent; 14.3%, to very large extent). The remaining of the respondents selected less importance of this factor during decision process.

The importance of risk as part of the influence factor in the decision process was acknowledged by 64.3% of the respondents (42.9%, to large extent; 21.4%, to very large extent). 21.4% of the respondents perceived to some extent and 7.1% of the respondents perceived to small extent. Only 7.1% of the respondents did not consider this factor at all.

Finally, the common limitation of SMEs in expanding their business due to size of the company was not perceived as important by majority of the respondents (50%, to small extent; 35.7%, to some extent). Only 14.3% of the respondents considered this factor during decision process.

5.2.5 Decision making method (Q2)

In this question, the respondents were asked to identify the decision making method they used most frequently in marketing process. Two options garnered the majority of responses. Approximately 71% of respondents chose informal method or combination of informal and formal method as their preferred decision making method. The second preferred decision method was strategic decision method (21.4%). The rest of the respondents specified their preferred method as formal decision method. Figure 5.2 shows the responses.

Figure 5.2: Proportion of decision making methods

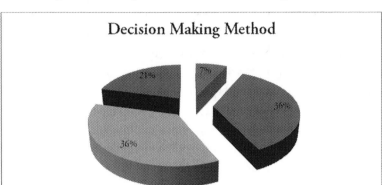

5.2.6 Source of information (Q3)

To gain further insight into the source of information in the process of making marketing decision, 15 information factors were included to facilitate the respondent to identify the importance of these sources based on the developed five-point Likert scales including "very unlikely", "unlikely", "neutral", "likely", and "very likely", as shown in Table 5.4.

About 64.8% (4.9%, very likely; 59.9%, likely) of the respondents perceived past experience as an important factor in marketing decision making process, while the remaining 14.3% selected neutral when asked to respond on past experience.

Table 5.4: Source of information

Source of information	Very unlikely	Unlikely	Neutral	Likely	Very likely	Mean	Std. Dev.
Past experience		19 (10.4%)	45 (24.7%)	109 (59.8%)	9 (4.9%)	3.59	0.7721
Formal education		13 (7.1%)	52 (28.6%)	117 (64.3%)		3.57	0.6244
Other business managers		13 (7.1%)	13 (7.1%)	156 (85.7%)		3.78	0.5594
Friend/social network		26 (14.3%)	26 (14.3%)	130 (71.4%)		3.57	0.7304
Customers		26 (14.3%)	13 (7.1%)	117 (64.3%)	26 (14.3%)	3.78	0.8624
Family		104 (57.1%)	65 (35.7%)	13 (7.1%)		2.50	0.6285
Media	13 (7.1%)	104 (57.1%)	26 (14.3%)	39 (21.4%)		2.50	0.9088
Suppliers		65 (35.7%)	39 (21.4%)	78 (21.4%)		3.07	0.8859
Internet	39 (21.4%)	65 (35.7%)	39 (21.4%)	39 (21.4%)		2.42	1.0526
External private sector consultant	26 (14.3%)	130 (71.4%)	26 (14.3%)			2.00	0.5360
Banks or other financial institutions	26 (14.3%)	143 (78.6%)	13 (7.1%)			1.92	0.4586
Seminars/ conference/ workshop	26 (14.3%)	117 (64.3%)	39 (21.4%)			2.28	0.9609
Marketing/ Trade exhibitions	13 (7.1%)	65 (35.7%)	26 (14.3%)	78 (42.9%)		2.92	1.035
Industry or SMEs associations	26 (14.3%)	65 (35.7%)	26 (14.3%)	65 (35.7%)		2.71	1.1003
Government (SME Corp, Matrade, etc.)	52 (28.6%)	39 (21.4%)	13 (7.1%)	78 (42.9%)		2.64	1.2912

Next, 64.3% of the respondents perceived that knowledge from formal education was very likely important in their marketing decision making process. Other than that, 7.1% of the respondents indicated that they were unlikely to apply the knowledge that they had learnt, while the remaining 28.6% of the respondents selected neutral to respond to the importance of formal education.

Moreover, in this survey, 85.7% of the respondents were likely to refer to other business manager for obtaining information and advice. Only 7.1% of the respondents were unlikely to use this source in their marketing decision making process. The remaining respondents (7.1%) selected neutral response for this source.

Next, majority of the respondents (71.4%) were likely to use typical SMEs networking such as friends and customers for information gathering. Only 14.3% of the respondents in this survey were unlikely to use this source of information, while the remaining (14.3%) selected neutral as their response.

Other than that, information fed from the family in marketing decision making was only perceived by 7.1% of the respondents. Majority of the respondents (57.1%) were unlikely to refer to their family in making the decision, while the remaining (35.7%) indicated neutral response to this source of information.

Next, majority of the respondents (7.1%, very unlikely; 57.1%, unlikely) in this survey rejected the media as a source of information. Only 21.4% of the respondents indicated that they were likely to use the source. The remaining of the respondents selected neutral as their response (14.3%).

One of the significant information sources indicated by the respondents in this survey was their supplier (21.4%, likely). However, majority of the respondents (35.7%, unlikely) did not use this source in making marketing decision making, while remaining 21.4% of the respondents selected neutral response to this source.

The relevance of trade exhibitions as a platform to explore the business opportunity was acknowledged by close to half of the respondents (42, 9% likely). This evidence shows the importance of this platform in SMEs environment, but more effort by relevant authorities is sought to educate the SMEs owner managers on the importance of this platform.

Next, the Internet was also one of the items evaluated by the respondents as their source of information in making marketing decision making. Majority of the respondents (21.4%, very unlikely; 35.7%, unlikely) indicated the awareness of the respondent to this technology as a source of information. Only (21.4%) of the respondents were likely to use this source of information. However, significant percentage of respondents (21.4%) selected neutral response, which probably indicated a minimum usage of Internet as a source of information.

Moreover, more than 78% of the respondents (14.3%, very unlikely; 71.4%, unlikely) rejected assistance from external private consultant. Only 7.1% of the respondents stated that they used external consultant service. The remaining 14.3% of the respondents selected neutral as their response.

Next, none of the respondents used information from banks or other financial institutions, and from seminars/conference/workshop.

Next, contribution from SMEs business associations was only used by 28.6% (likely) of the respondents. Majority of the respondents (7.1%, very unlikely; 50% unlikely) were unlikely to use this source of information.

Finally, only 42.9% of the respondents had sought assistance from the Government in making their marketing decision. Majority of the respondents (28.6%, very unlikely; 21.4%, unlikely) indicated no interest on the assistance from this source of information.

5.2.7   Decision Outcome (Q4)

In this question, respondents were asked about the effectiveness of decision outcome. Majority of the respondents in this survey were satisfied with the outcome of their decision, as illustrated in Table 5.5. This finding supports the findings from the qualitative survey that decision makers are rational in selecting the most suitable method to achieve the desired outcome.

Table 5.5: Decision outcome effectiveness

Question	Strongly disagree	Disagree	Neutral	Agree	Strongly agree	Mean	Std. Dev.
We are very satisfied, everything went as planned				47 (25.8%)	135 (74.2%)	4.7418	.43887
We are satisfied, even though we have experienced minor complication			12 (6.6%)	59 (32.4%)	111 (60.9%)	4.5440	.61809
Nothing has changed, no improvements are seen	106 (58.2%)	63 (34.6%)	13 (7.2%)			1.4890	.62842
We are not satisfied, our goals have not been fulfilled	153 (84%)	17 (9.4%)	12 (6.6%)			1.2253	.55506

5.3   Inferential Analysis

The information attained from the descriptive analysis has provided us with general information regarding the current status of the research subject. However, this information is not sufficient to report various issues in the process of making marketing decision. For this reason, additional statistical analysis reporting is needed to address the following subresearch questions:

- Research question 1

  Do these factors (driving factors) significantly influence the decision outcome?

- Research question 2

  Are there any significant differences in adoption on sources of information based on the decision maker's characteristics (gender, age, ethnicity, and education level)?

- Research question 3

  Are there any significant differences in the adoption of decision method based on the decision maker's characteristics (gender, age, ethnicity, and education level)?

- Research question 4

  Are there any significant relationships between the decision method and the decision outcome?

5.3.1 Research Question 1 (Ho1)

The null hypothesis was as follows: *There is a relationship between the driving factor and the decision outcome.*

In this section, standard multiple regressions were used to investigate the influence of driving factor to the decision outcome, and to test the null hypothesis Ho1. According to Pallant (2005), there are three steps in analysing results using the standard multiple regression technique. They are checking the assumptions, evaluating the model, and evaluating each of independent variables.

Step 1: Checking the assumptions

Before using the standard multiple regression technique to analyse the result, assumptions of multiple regressions were tested as follows:

a) Sample size

Tabachnick and Fidell (2011) provide a formula for calculating sample size requirements by taking into account the number of independent variables. The formula is as follows:

Formula of sample size = N > 50 + 8m
(m = number of independent variables)

Based on the formula, 154 respondents were required for each independent variable. This indicated that the sample size of 182 in this study was sufficient to meet the standard regression requirement.

b) Outliers were checked using Mahalanobis distance tests using the multiple regression programs. The maximum score from the test was 27.782, as shown in Table 5.12.

Critical value for evaluating the Mahalanobis distance values in this study was adopted from Tabachnick and Fidell (2011) and Pallant (2005). There were 12 independent variables as shown in Table 5.6. Therefore, the critical value was 26.22.

Table 5.6: Outlier Residual Statistics

	Minimum	Maximum	Mean	Std. Deviation	N
Predicted Value	13.6091	18.2014	16.2143	1.28921	182
Std. Predicted Value	-2.021	1.541	.000	1.000	182
Standard Error of Predicted Value	.143	.337	.231	.039	182
Adjusted Predicted Value	13.5947	18.2758	16.2135	1.29608	182
Residual	-2.29728	2.28676	.00000	.81358	182
Std. Residual	-2.720	2.708	.000	.963	182
Stud. Residual	-2.794	2.774	.000	.998	182
Deleted Residual	-2.42375	2.39974	.00074	.87291	182
Stud. Deleted Residual	-2.853	2.831	.001	1.004	182
Mahal. Distance	4.176	27.782	12.929	4.717	182
Cook's Distance	.000	.035	.005	.006	182
Centred Leverage Value	.023	.153	.071	.026	182

a. Dependent Variable: Decision Outcome

c) Normal P-P plot of regression standardised residual

Figure 5.3 shows a normal plot of the regression standardised residual. This indicates that the data were appropriate to be used in the multiple regression analysis because the residuals showed a straight line (from bottom left to top right) relationship with the predicted dependent variable scores.

Figure 5.3: Normal P-P Plot of Regression Standardised Residual

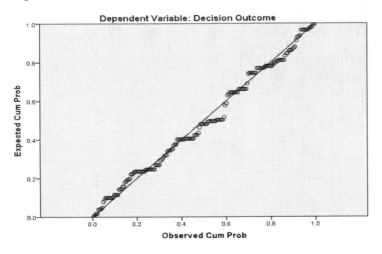

d) Histogram

Figure 5.4 confirms that the data were suitable to be used in the multiple regression analysis because the residuals were normally distributed about the predicted dependent scores.

Figure 5.4: Histogram

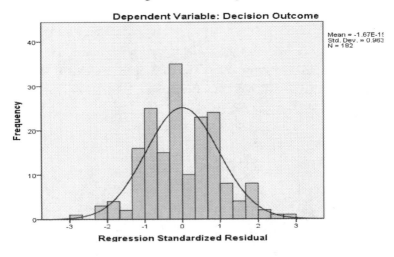

e) Collinearity diagnostics

Table 5.7 shows the results of tolerance and VIF. Generally, cut-off points for determining the presence of multicollinearity are a tolerance value of less than .10 and VIF value of above 10. In this present study, the tolerance value for each independent variable was more than .10, and these results were supported by the VIF values, which were below 10. Therefore, the results indicated that there was no violation of multicollinearity assumption.

Table 5.7: Coefficient

Model	Standardised Coefficients	t	Sig.	Collinearity Statistics	
	Beta			Tolerance	VIF
(Constant)		32.850	.000		
Personal vision	.276	2.477	.000	.137	7.314
Personal competency	−.533	−4.290	.000	.110	9.106
Long-term business relationship	.110	1.655	.000	.386	2.591
Goal setting	−.458	−4.486	.000	.162	6.158
Personal and lifestyle consideration	.050	1.042	.000	.724	1.381
Ethical and social consideration	−.065	−1.245	.000	.631	1.585
Personal experience	−.238	−4.294	.000	.553	1.809
Financial return	.806	9.609	.000	.241	4146
Company financial capability	.661	7.427	.000	.214	4.668
Market size	.280	3.657	.000	.290	3.449
Risk size	−.714	−6.617	.000	.146	6.870
Size of company	−.717	−7.373	.000	.179	5.586

a. Dependent Variable: Decision Outcome

Step 2: Evaluating the model

Results of R square shown in Table 5.8 indicate how much of the variance in the dependent variable (decision outcome) is explained by the model (which includes the 12 independent variables). In this study, the value of adjusted R square was .717. When expressed as a percentage multiplied by 100, this means that the model explained 71.7% of the variance in frequency of decision outcome.

Table 5.8: Model sumamry

Model	R	R Square	Adjusted R Square	Std. Error of the Estimate
1	.846[a]	.717	.693	.84801

a. Predictors: (Constant), Personal vision, Personal competency, Past experience, Long-term Business relationship, Goal setting, Personal and lifestyle consideration, Personal experience, Financial return, Company financial capability, Market size, Risk size, Size of company
b. Dependent variable: Decision outcome

Furthermore, to asses the statistical significance of the result (see Table 5.9) for testing that multiple R in the population was equal to 0, the model in this study reached statistical significance [$F_{(13,166)}$ = 32.155, $p < 0.000$].

Table 5.9: ANOVA

Model		Sum of Squares	df	Mean Square	F	Sig.
1	Regression	300.603	13	23.123	32.155	.000[a]
	Residual	119.375	166	.719		
	Total	419.978	179			

a. Predictors: (Constant), Personal vision, Personal competency, Past experience, Long-term Business relationship, Goal setting, Personal and lifestyle consideration, Personal experience, Financial return, Company financial capability, Market size, Risk size, Size of company

b. Dependent variable: Decision making outcome.

Step 3: Evaluating each of the independent variables

This section discusses which of the 12 independent variables included in the model contributed to the predication of dependent variable (decision making method). Results (see Table 5.7) show that all the variables ($p < .05$) made a significant contribution to the prediction of the dependent variable (decision outcome). Furthermore, the beta coefficient value used standardised coefficient rather than unstandardised coefficient because, as emphasised by Pallant (2005), these values have been converted to the same scale so that the results can be compared to each of the different variables. Results (see Table 5.7) indicate that the independent variable namely financial return was the largest beta coefficient (Beta = 0.806). This means that this independent variable made the strongest contribution to explain the dependent variable. In other words, financial return was the best factor that influenced the decision outcome throughout the process.

Therefore, the null hypothesis Ho1 stating *There is a relationship between the driving factor and the decision outcome* was accepted.

5.3.2   Research Question 2 (Ho2, HHHHH Ho3, Ho4, Ho5)

For this research question, four null hypotheses (Ho2 to H05) were tested to identify the significant difference in adoption of source of information based on the decision maker's characteristics (gender, age, ethnicity, and education level).

1.   Gender (Ho2)

The null hypothesis was as follows: *There is a significant difference among the genders of SMEs decision makers in adoption of source of information.*

An independent samples t-test was conducted to compare the adoption of source of information between the gender of SME decision maker as shown in Table 5.10 and Table 5.11. There was a significant difference in the score for male ($M=42.5$ $SD=6.316$) and for female ($M=47.9$, $SD=3.61$) conditions; t (180) = 4.227, p = 0.00, P<.05. Results indicated that the difference in gender does have an effect on adoption source of information. Specifically, the finding shows that the level adoption of source information is different between male or female decision makers.

Table 5.10: Group Statistic

	Gender	N	Mean	Std. Deviation	Std. Error Mean
Source of information	Male	156	42.5385	6.31678	.50575
	Female	26	47.9231	3.61024	.70803

Table 5.11: Independent Sample Test

		Levene's Test for Equality of Variances		t-test for Equality of Means							
										95% Confidence Interval of the Difference	
		F	Sig.	t	df	Sig. (2-tailed)	Mean Difference	Std. Error Difference		Lower	Upper
Source of Information	Equal variances assumed	2.629	.107	-4.227	180	.000	-5.38462	1.27398		-7.89847	-2.87077
	Equal variances not assumed			-6.188	54.722	.000	-5.38462	.87010		-7.12854	-3.64069

In summary, there is a statistically significant mean difference in making marketing decision between males and females. Results show that female decision maker tends to be more resources in adoption the source of information than male decision maker. Therefore, the null hypothesis Ho2: stating *There is a significant difference among the genders of SMEs decision makers in adoption of source of information* was accepted.

2. Age (Ho3)

The null hypothesis was as follows: *There is a significant difference among the ages of SMEs decision makers in adoption of source of information.*

One-way analysis of variance (ANOVA) was conducted to explore whether there was a significant difference in the mean scores on the dependent variable "source of information" in the ages of decision makers. Table 5.12 reveals the results of the assumptions underlying the analysis of variance. The value of p = 0.01 (significance value less than .01) from the test of the null hypothesis indicated that the variance of the dependent variable was not equal across the independent variable. Thus, it can be concluded that there was violation in the homogeneity of variances assumption.

Table 5.12: Test of Homogeneity of Variances

Dependent variable: Source of information

Levene Statistics	df1	df2	Sig.
11.986	1	180	.001

Having noted that the assumption of homogeneity of variance was not affected, or only slightly affected, the result was valid (Weinberg and Abramowitz, 2002: Pallant, 2005). An alternative test, Robust Test of Equality of Means (Welsh and Brown-Forsythe) may be used when the assumption of the homogeneity of variance is violated (Pallant 2005). In this study, results from the Robust Test of Equality of Means (see Table 5.13) and test of between-subject effect (see Table 5.14 both revealed the same significant value (p = 0.000), confirming that the ANOVA analysis still provided a valid test result. Therefore, the significant value result from the test of between-subject effect (see Table 5.14) was used in order to test the null hypothesis (Ho2).

Table 5.13: Robust Tests of Equality of Means

Dependent variable: Source of information

	Statistics[a]	df1	df2	Sig.
Welch	73.787	1	174.715	.000
Brown-Forsythe	73.787	1	174.715	.000

a. Asymptotically F distributed.

As shown in Table 5.14 (test of between-subject effect), the result shows that there is a statistically significant difference at p < 0.001 level for adoption of source of information among the ages of decision maker [F(1,180) = 74.212, p = 0.000]. The actual difference in mean scores (see Table 5.15) between group indicated a large effect (ETA = .292).

Table 5.14: Test of Between-Subject Effect

Dependent variable: Source of information

	Sum of Squares	df	Mean Square	F	Sig.	Eta Squared
Between Groups	2079.238	1	2079.238	74.212	.000	.292
Within Groups	5043.136	180	28.017			
Total	7122.374	181				

Table 5.15: Test of Means Difference

Dependent variable: Source of information

Age	Mean	N	Std. Deviation
Less than 40 years old	46.7079	89	5.613512
Between 40 and 55 years old	39.9462	93	4.94396
Total	43.2527	182	6.27297

In summary, the difference in ages did affect the adoption on source of information among the SMEs decision makers. Therefore, the null hypothesis Ho3 was accepted.

3. Ethnicity (Ho4)

The null hypothesis was as follows: *There is a significant difference among the ethnicities of SMEs decision makers in the adoption of source of information.*

One-way analysis of variance (ANOVA) was conducted to explore whether there was a significant difference in the mean scores on the dependent variable "decision making method" among the ethnicities. Table 5.16 reveals the results of the assumptions underlying the analysis of variance. The significance of p = 0.00 (significance value less than .05) from the test of the null hypothesis indicated that the variance of the dependent variable was not equal across the independent variable. Thus, it can be concluded that there was violation in the homogeneity of variances assumption.

Table 5.16: Test of Homogeneity of Variances

Dependent variable: Source of information

Levene Statistics	df1	df2	Sig.
32.086	2	179	.000

However, results from the Robust Tests of Equality of Means (see Table 5.17) and test of between-subject effect (see Table 5.18) both revealed the same significant value (p = 0.000), confirming that ANOVA analysis still provided a valid test result. Therefore, the significant value result from the test of between-subject effect (see Table 5.18) was used in order to test the null hypothesis (Ho1).

Table 5.17: Robust Tests of Equality of Means

Dependent variable: Source of information

	Statistics[a]	df1	df2	Sig.
Welch	39.000	2	112.384	.000
Brown-Forsythe	65.036	2	168.119	.000

a. Asymptotically F distributed.

In this study, the result for between-subject effect test showed that there is a statistically significant difference at p < .001 level for adoption of source of information among the ethnicities [F(2,179) = 33.151, p = .000]. The eta-squared value (.270) indicated a large effect of size. This result is illustrated in Table 5.19.

Table 5.18: Test of Between-Subject Effects

Dependent variable: Source of information

	Sum of Squares	df	Mean Square	F	Sig.	Eta Squared
Between Groups	1925.074	2	962.537	33.151	.000	.270
Within Groups	5197.299	179	29.035			
Total	7122.374	181				

Table 5.19: Test of Means Difference

Dependent variable: Source of information

Race	Mean	N	Std. Deviation
Malay	46.0588	102	6.70425
Chinese	38.9074	54	3.37733
Indian	41.2692	26	1.45761
Total	43.2527	182	6.27297

The post-hoc multiple comparisons test (Tukey HSD) was used to test the significant difference of mean scores between groups. Results (see Table 5.20) reveal that there were significant differences in the adoption of information sources between Malay and Chinese, and between Malay and India at $p < 0.05$ level.

Table 5.20: Post-Hoc Multiple Comparisons Test (Tukey HSD) (Adoption of information among the ethnicities)

Dependent variable: Source of information

(I) Race	(J) Race	Mean Difference (I-J)	Std. Error	Sig.
Malay	Chinese	7.15142*	.90683	.000
	Indian	4.78959*	1.18381	.000
Chinese	Malay	-7.15142*	.90683	.000
	Indian	-2.36182	1.28625	.161
Indian	Malay	-4.78959*	1.18381	.000
	Chinese	2.36182	1.28625	.161

*. The mean difference is significant at the 0.05 level.

In summary, the difference between ethnicities did affect the adoption of information among SME's decision makers. Therefore, the null hypothesis Ho4 stating *There is a significant difference among the ethnicities of SMEs decision makers in the adoption of source of information* was accepted.

4. Education (Ho5)

The null hypothesis was *There is a significant difference among the education levels of SMEs decision makers in the adoption of source of information.*

One-way analysis of variance (ANOVA) was conducted to explore whether there was a significant difference in the mean scores on the dependent variable "source of information" among the levels of education. Table 5.21 reveals results of the assumptions underlying analysis of variance. The significance of $p = 0.00$ (significance value less than .05) from the test of the null hypothesis indicated that the variance of the dependent variable was not equal across the independent variable. Thus, it can be concluded that there was violation in the homogeneity of variances assumption.

Table 5.21: Test of Homogeneity of Variances

Dependent variable: Source of information

Levene Statistics	df1	df2	Sig.
15.950	3	178	.000

However, results from the Robust Tests of Equality of Means (see Table 5.22) and test of between-subject effect (see Table 5.23) both revealed the same significant value ($p = 0.000$), confirming that the ANOVA analysis still provided a valid test result. Therefore, the significant value from the test of between-subject effect (see Table 5.23) was used in order to test the null hypothesis (Ho4).

Table 5.22: Robust Tests of Equality of Means

Dependent variable: Source of information

	Statistics[a]	df1	df2	Sig.
Welch	32.128	3	66.647	.000
Brown-Forsythe	29.208	3	137.150	.000

a. Asymptotically F distributed

In this study, test between subject effect showed that there was a statistically significant difference at p < .001 level for source of information among the different levels of education [F(3,178) = 17,701, p = .000]. The eta-squared value (.230) indicated a large effect of size.

Table 5.23: Test of Between-Subject Effect

Dependent variable: Source of information

	Sum of Squares	df	Mean Square	F	Sig.	Eta Squared
Between Groups	1636.565	3	545.522	17.701	.000	.230
Within Groups	5485.809	178	30.819			
Total	7122.374	181				

Table 5.24: Test of Means Difference

Dependent variable: Source of information

Highest education level	Mean	N	Std. Deviation
High school	40.6923	26	.61769
Diploma	46.5789	38	5.05447
Bachelor's Degree	44.3667	90	6.86049
Master's Degree	37.3077	26	3.69615
Total	43.2833	180	6.30090

The post-hoc multiple comparisons test (Tukey HSD) was used to test the significant differences of mean scores between groups. Table 5.25 confirms that there were significant differences (mean scores) for the adoption of source of information based on education level between Master's degree and diploma, and between Master's degree and Bachelor's degree at p < .05 level

Table 5.25: Post-hoc Multiple Comparisons Test (Tukey HSD) (Adoption of decision making method based on education level)

Source of information

(I) Highest education level	(J) Highest education level	Mean Difference (I-J)	Std. Error	Sig.
High school	Diploma	−5.90038*	1.38265	.000
	Bachelor's degree	−3.68810*	1.20130	.013
	Master's degree	3.37088	1.51196	.119
Diploma	High school	5.90038*	1.38265	.000
	Bachelor's degree	2.21228	1.07400	.170
	Master's degree	9.27126*	1.41293	.000
Bachelor's degree	High school	3.68810*	1.20130	.013
	Diploma	−2.21228	1.07400	.170
	Master's degree	7.05897*	1.23604	.000
Master's degree	High school	3.37088	1.51196	.119
	Diploma	−9.27126*	1.41293	.000
	Bachelor's degree	−7.05897*	1.23604	.000

*. The mean difference is significant at the 0.05 level.

In summary, results in this study indicated that level of education did affect the adoption on source of information. Therefore, the null hypothesis Ho5 stating *There is a significant difference among the education levels of SMEs decision makers in the adoption of source of information* was accepted.

5.3.3 Research Question 3 (Ho6, Ho7, Ho8, Ho9)

For this research question, four null hypotheses (Ho6 to Ho9) were tested for the identification of significant difference in adoption of decision method based on the decision maker's characteristics (gender, age, ethnicity, and education level).

1. Gender (Ho6)

The null hypothesis was as follows: *There is a significant difference among the genders of SMEs decision makers in adoption of decision method.*

One-way analysis of variance (ANOVA) was conducted to explore whether there was a significant difference in the mean scores on the dependent variable "adoption of decision method" in making marketing decision between males and females. Table 5.26 reveals results of the assumptions underlying analysis of variance. The significance of $p = 0.04$ (significance value less than .05) from the test of the null hypothesis indicated that the variance of the dependent variable was not equal across the independent variable. Thus, it can be concluded that there was violation in the homogeneity of variances assumption.

Table 5.26: Test of Homogeneity of Variances

Dependent variable: Decision making method

Levene Statistics	df1	df2	Sig.
8.581	1	180	.004

However, results from the Robust Test of Equality of Means (see Table 5.27) and test of between-subject effect (see Table 5.28) both revealed the same significant value ($p = 0.000$), confirming that the ANOVA analysis still provided a valid test result. Therefore, the significant value result from the test of between-subject effect (see Table 5.28) was used in order to test the null hypothesis (Ho6)

Table 5.27: Robust Tests of Equality of Means

Dependent variable: Decision making method

	Statistics[a]	df1	df2	Sig.
Welch	53.523	1	49.326	.000
Brown-Forsythe	53.523	1	49.326	.000

a. Asymptotically F distributed

In Table 5.28 (test of between-subject effect), the result shows that there is a statistically significant difference at $p < 0.001$ level for adoption of source of information among the ages of decision maker [$F(1,180) = 25.691$, $p = 0.000$]. The actual difference in mean scores (see Table 5.29) between group indicated a medium effect (ETA = .125).

Table 5.28: Test of Between-Subject Effect

Dependent variable: Decision making method

	Sum of Squares	df	Mean Square	F	Sig.	Eta Squared
Between Groups	17.483	1	17.483	25.691	.000	.125
Within Groups	122.495	180	.681			
Total	139.978	181				

Table 5.29: Test of Means Difference

Dependent variable: Decision making method

Gender	Mean	N	Std. Deviation
Male	2.5796	157	0.86326
Female	3.4800	25	0.50990
Total	2.7033	182	0.87941

In summary, the difference in gender did affect the adoption on source of information among SME's decision maker. Therefore, the null hypothesis Ho6 stating *There is a significant difference among the genders of SMEs decision makers in adoption of decision method* was accepted.

2. Age (Ho7)

The null hypothesis was as follows: *There is a significant difference among the ages of SMEs decision makers in adoption of decision method.*

One-way analysis of variance (ANOVA) was conducted to explore whether there was a significant difference in the mean scores on the dependent variable "adoption of decision method" according to age of the decision makers. Table 5.30 reveals the results of the assumptions underlying the analysis of variance. The significance of p = 0.497 (significance value more than .05) from the test of the null hypothesis indicated that the variance of the dependent variable was equal across the independent variable. Thus, it can be concluded that there was no violation in the homogeneity of variances assumption.

Table 5.30: Test of Homogeneity of Variances

Dependent variable: Decision making method

Levene Statistics	df1	df2	Sig.
.464	1	180	.497

In Table 5.31 (test of between-subject effect), the result shows that there is a statistically significant difference at p < 0.001 level for the adoption of decision making method in the process of making marketing decision among the ages of decision makers [F(1,180) = 5.230, p = 0.000]. The actual difference in mean scores (see Table 5.32) between group was indicated as medium effect of size (eta-squared value = .028).

Table 5.31: Test of Between-Subject Effect

Dependent variable: Decision making method

	Sum of Squares	df	Mean Square	F	Sig.	Eta Squared
Between Groups	3.592	1	3.952	5.230	.000	.028
Within Groups	136.026	180	0.756			
Total	139.978	181				

Table 5.32: Test of Means Difference

Dependent variable: Decision making method

Age	Mean	N	Std. Deviation
Less than 40 years old	2.8539	89	0.83327
Between 40 and 55 years old	2.5591	93	0.90244
Total	2.7033	182	0.87941

In summary, the difference in ages did affect the adoption of decision method of the persons responsible in making marketing decision. Therefore, the null hypothesis Ho7 stating *There is a significant difference among the ages of SMEs decision makers in adoption of decision method* was accepted.

3. Ethnicity (Ho8)

The null hypothesis was as follows: *There is a significant difference among the ethnicities of SMEs decision makers in the adoption of decision method.*

One-way analysis of variance (ANOVA) was conducted to explore whether there was a significant difference in the mean scores on the dependent variable "decision making method" among the ethnicities. Table 5.33 reveals the results of the assumptions underlying the analysis of variance. The significance of p = 0.01 (significance value less than .05) from the test of the null hypothesis indicated that the variance of the dependent variable was not equal across the independent variable. Thus, it can be concluded that there was violation in the homogeneity of variances assumption.

Table 5.33: Test of Homogeneity of Variances

Dependent variable: Decision making method

Levene Statistics	df1	df2	Sig.
7.802	2	179	.001

However, results from the Robust Tests of Equality of Means (see Table 5.34) and test of between-subject effect (see Table 5.35) both revealed the same significant value (p = 0.000), confirming that ANOVA analysis still provided a valid test result. Therefore, the significant value result from the test of between-subject effect (see Table 5.35) was used in order to test the null hypothesis (Ho8).

Table 5.34: Robust Tests of Equality of Means

Dependent variable: Decision making method

	Statistics[a]	df1	df2	Sig.
Welch	126.226	2	71.017	.000
Brown-Forsythe	147.873	2	110.553	.000

a. Asymptotically F distributed

In this study, test of between-subject effect showed that there was a statistically significant difference at p < .001 level for decision making method among the ethnicities [F(2,179) = 120.119, p = .000]. The eta-squared value (.573) indicated a large effect of size.

Table 5.35: Test of Between-Subject Effect

Dependent variable: Decision making method

	Sum of Squares	df	Mean Square	F	Sig.	Eta Squared
Between Groups	80.235	2	40.118	120.199	.000	.573
Within Groups	59.743	179	0.334			
Total	139.978	181				

The actual difference in mean scores (see Table 5.36) indicated significant difference among the groups as follows: Malay (55.78), Chinese (51.75), and Indian (46.62). This finding indicated that driving factor among the ethnicities significantly influenced the decision making process.

Table 5.36: Test of Means Difference

Dependent variable: Decision making method

Race	Mean	N	Std. Deviation
Malay	3.2549	102	0.65531
Chinese	2.2407	54	0.43155
Indian	1.50000	26	0.50990
Total	2.7033	182	0.87941

The post-hoc multiple comparisons test (Tukey HSD) was used to test the significant differences of mean scores between groups. Table 5.37 confirms that there were significant differences (mean scores) for the adoption of decision making method among the ethnicities at $p < .05$ level.

Hairul Rizad and Abu Bakar

Table 5.37: Post-hoc Multiple Comparisons Test (Tukey HSD)
(Adoption of decision making method among the ethnicities)

Dependent variable: Decision making method

(I) Race	(J) Race	Mean Difference (I-J)	Std. Error	Sig.
Malay	Chinese	1.01416*	.09723	.000
	Indian	1.75490*	.12692	.000
Chinese	Malay	–1.01416*	.09723	.000
	Indian	.74074*	.13790	.000
Indian	Malay	–1.75490*	.12692	.000
	Chinese	–.74074*	.13790	.000

*. The mean difference is significant at the 0.05 level.

In summary, the results indicated that difference in ethnicities did affect the adoption of decision making method during the process of making marketing decision. Therefore, the null hypothesis Ho8 stating *There is a significant difference among the ethnicities of SMEs decision makers in the adoption of decision method* was accepted.

4. Education (Ho9)

The null hypothesis was as follows: *There is a significant difference among the education levels of SMEs decision makers in the adoption of decision method.*

One-way analysis of variance (ANOVA) was conducted to explore whether there was a significant difference in the mean scores on the dependent variable "decision making method" and the education level received by the decision makers. Table 5.38 reveals the results of the assumptions underlying the analysis of variance. The significance of $p = 0.00$ (significance value less than .05) from the test of the null hypothesis indicated that the variance of the dependent variable was not equal across the independent variable.

Thus, it can be concluded that there was violation in the homogeneity of variances assumption.

Table 5.38: Test of Homogeneity of Variances

Dependent variable: Decision making method

Levene Statistics	df1	df2	Sig.
84.327	3	178	.000

However, results from the Robust Tests of Equality of Means (see Table 5.39) and test of between-subject effect (see Table 5.40) both revealed significantly different values.

Table 5.39: Robust Tests of Equality of Means

Dependent variable: Decision making method

	Statistics[a]	df1	df2	Sig.
Welch	5.574	3	41.758	.000
Brown-Forsythe	1.790	3	32.138	.000

a. Asymptotically F distributed.

The test between-subject effect showed that there was statistically significant difference at $p < .001$ level for decision method factor among the education levels [$F (3,178) = 9.951$, $p = .000$]. The eta-squared value (.144) indicated a large effect of education level to the decision makers.

Table 5.40: Test of Between-Subject Effects

Dependent variable: Decision making method

	Sum of Squares	df	Mean Square	F	Sig.	Eta Squared
Between Groups	20.104	3	6.701	9.9951	.000	.144
Within Groups	119.874	178	0.673			
Total	139.978	181				

Table 5.41: Test of Means Difference

Dependent variable: Decision making method

Highest education level	Mean	N	Std. Deviation
High school	2.0000	28	0.0000
Diploma	2.9737	38	1.44235
Bachelor's Degree	2.8667	90	.63952
Master's Degree	2.5000	26	.50990
Total	2.7111	182	.88114

The post-hoc multiple comparisons test (Tukey HSD) was used to test the significant differences of mean scores between groups. Table 5.42 confirms that there were significant differences (mean scores) for the adoption on decision making method based on education level between high school and diploma, and between high school and bachelor's degree at $p < .05$ level.

Table 5.42: Post-hoc Multiple Comparisons Test (Tukey HSD)
(Adoption of decision method based on education level)

Dependent variable: Decision making method

(I) Highest education level	(J) Highest education level	Mean Difference (I-J)	Std. Error	Sig.
High school	Diploma	–.97368	.21005	.000
	Bachelor's degree	–.86667	.18375	.000
	Master's degree	–.50000	.22889	.132
Diploma	High school	.97368	.21005	.000
	Bachelor's degree	–.10702	.15966	.908
	Master's degree	.47368	.21005	.113
Bachelor's degree	High school	.86667	.18375	.000
	Diploma	–.10702	.15966	.908
	Master's degree	.36667	.18375	.194
Master's degree	High school	.50000	.22889	.132
	Diploma	–.47368	.21005	.113
	Bachelor's degree	–.36667	.18375	.194

*. The mean difference is significant at the 0.05 level.

In summary, the results indicated that difference in education level did affect the adoption of decision making method during the process of making marketing decision. Therefore, the null hypothesis Ho9 stating *There is a significant difference among the education levels of SMEs decision makers in the adoption of decision method* was accepted.

5.3.4 Research Question 4 (Ho10)

The null hypothesis was as follows: *There is a relationship between the decision method used in the decision making process and the decision outcome.*

5.3.4.1 Correlation analysis

For the research question 4, correlation analysis was employed to examine the relationships between independent variable and dependent variable, as shown in Table 5.43. The score of correlation between decision method and decision outcome was .381, and the relationship was negatively significant at $p < 0.01$ ($p = 0.000$).

Table 5.43: The Result of Correlation Analysis for the Dependent Variables (Decision Outcome) and Independent Variables (Decision Making Method)

Variable	Correlation	Decision making method
	Pearson Correlation	−.381
Decision outcome	Sig. (1-tailed)	.000
	N	182

5.3.4.2 Standard Regression Analysis

Results of R square shown in Table 5.44 indicate how far the variance in the dependent variable (decision outcome) is explained by the independent variables (decision making method). In this study, the value of adjusted R square was .140. When expressed as a percentage multiplied by 100, this means that the model explains 14 per cent of the variance in frequency of decision outcome.

Table 5.44: Model sumamry

Model	R	R Square	Adjusted R Square	Std. Error of the Estimate
1	.381[a]	.145	.140	1.42025

a. Predictors: (Constant), Decision making method

b. Dependent Variable: Decision outcome

The model in this study reached statistical significance [$F(1,110)$ = 18.690, p < 0.000].

Table 5.45: ANOVA

Model		Sum of Squares	df	Mean Square	F	Sig.
1	Regression	61.090	1	61.090	30.583	.000[a]
	Residual	359.553	180	1.998		
	Total	420.643	181			

a. Predictors: (Constant), Decision making method

b. Dependent Variable: Decision outcome

The regression coefficient indicates a significant relationship at p < 0.000, as illustrated in Table 5.46.

Table 5.46: Regression Coefficient

Model		Standardised Coefficients	t	Sig.
		Beta		
1	(Constant)		53.024	.000
	Decision making method	–.381	–5.530	.000

a. Dependent Variable: Decision outcome

Therefore, the null hypothesis (Ho10) stating *There is a relationship between the decision method used in the decision making process and the decision outcome* was accepted.

5.4   Summary

This chapter reports the analysis of the survey data resulting in a description of the process in making marketing decision by SMEs in Malaysia and insight into the factors driving the process. This chapter starts with a descriptive analysis of demographic data, followed by an examination of SMEs marketing decision process using a series of statistical tests on the relationship posited in Chapter 2. The finding of process in making marketing decision by SME can be described as limited using quantitative analysis, and thus further analysis by qualitative is needed to provide insight into SMEs current practice in making marketing decision. Chapter 6 provides further discussion about the findings.

CHAPTER 6

DISCUSSION, IMPLICATION AND CONCLUSION

6.0 Introduction

This chapter provides discussion, implication, and conclusion of this thesis. The discussion is organised according to research question, and findings are put together in context of current academic knowledge. The chapter begins by discussing the results in relation of four research questions. This is followed by discussion on a model of SME marketing decision making process. Next, this chapter also presents the implication of the finding for practice and policy that may be of interest to academic researchers, policy makers, and practitioners. Limitations associated with the present study and recommendations for future research are provided next. Lastly, the chapter concludes with a summary of contribution of this study to extend the knowledge on SME marketing.

6.1 Discussion on Research Question 1

6.1.1 Discussion on "What are the driving factors considered in the decision making process?"

12 driving factors influencing the SMEs decision makers, namely personal vision, personal competency, long-term business relationship, goal setting, personal and lifestyle consideration, ethical and social consideration, personal experience, financial return (profit

margin), company financial capability, market size, risk size, and size of the company were identified and evaluated.

According to Marleen (2010), SMEs decision makers' personal vision can be described as critical in the firm's decision. It implies how the SMEs owner managers foresee the benefits, opportunity, or risk of the decision. In the qualitative study, only two respondents namely from Company C & Company D acknowledged the importance of personal vision. However, there are differences found between these companies, i.e., in terms of vision and actual outcome. Differences in the SMEs decision makers' capabilities could explain the gap between the vision and the actual outcome. This finding was supported in the quantitative survey as 70% of the respondents acknowledged this factor (35%, to large extent; 35%, to very large extent). This finding supports Marleen's (2010) argument that SMEs decision makers are visionary are they are willing to take any risks in return of earning the benefit.

Personal competency is important to the decision makers as it demonstrates significant differences in trait characteristics such as risk taking, initiative, and independence. These attributes are more profound to SMEs owner managers than to professional managers in influencing decision outcome (Lee, 2012). In this study, personal competency was acknowledged by all the respondents in the qualitative study. Personal competency, even though only acknowledged by 71% of the respondents in quantitative study (57%, to large extent; 14%, to very large extent), was still a good indicator to differentiate the capability of SMEs decision makers with other professional managers. Previous studies also found significant positive correlations between individuals' competency and decision making performance (Hill *et al.*, 2001; Collis, 2010; Kristina, 2012). According to Kristina (2012), a competent SME decision maker should not only possess strategic thinking, ability to analyse the situation, and correctly perceive the information received, but also the talent to apply everything in practice.

Long-term business relationship has long been associated with the SME marketing characteristic (O'Dyer, 2010). SMEs with short-term business view mainly rely on profits in transaction, whereas SMEs with a long business view rely more on relational exchanges to maximise their profits over a series of transaction. Successful SMEs will consistently improve the relationship with the customers (Elaine, 2007). However, in the qualitative study, only one respondent acknowledged the importance of long-term business relationship. The decision maker from the Company D stated that "...*certainly cost is a major factor but this factor (long-term business relationship) is also equally important.*" This finding implies that other important factors are also considered by SMEs decision makers. Thus, this finding supports Uma and Bhuvaness's (2011) argument that SMEs decision makers always consider profitability above any other factors for the survival of their firm. This finding was further supported by the finding in quantitative study. 64% of the respondents acknowledged the importance of this factor, while 35% of the respondents acknowledged to some extent only.

Goal setting is the first step in decision making to ensure the company's goal is clear, specific, and unambiguous so that there will be no mistake during initiating the decision (Robert, 2002). In qualitative study of this present research, goal setting was acknowledged by only one decision maker (Company C), compared to 64.3% of the respondents in quantitative study who acknowledged the large extent of this factor to the decision making process. Thus, this finding did not supports Robert's (2002) and O'Dwyer's (2010) argument that marketing is often misunderstood by the SMEs.

In this study, only one respondent (Company A) from qualitative study and 14.3% of the respondents in quantitative study acknowledge the importance of personal lifestyle as an important factor in decision making process. This factor, which reflects a decision maker's personal interests and opinion to achieve social status through business, is still not common for most of the SMEs decision makers in this study.

Individuals who prioritise beliefs and knowledge in making decisions may also attempt to incorporate ethical and social consideration into their decision making process. According to Goodpaster (2004), ideologies are the bridge between values and decision making. Accordingly, if ethical and social consideration is included in the ideology of the SMEs decision makers, a greater likelihood exists that the decisions will be made more often to include ethical and social consideration. This is as informed by the decision maker the Company C who state that, "*I have a vision to expand my business and China is one of the good places to start as we face fierce competition locally. However, I'll not compromise business ethics during the process.*" The influence of this factor in the decision making process is significant in quantitative study where 64% of the respondents acknowledged the importance of this factor (42.9%, to large extent; 21.4%, to very large extent).

There is an extensive support in the literature on the effect of experience of the decision makers on their decision making method (Rocha, de Mello, Pacheco, & de Abreu Farias, 2012; Nielsen & Nielsen, 2010; Gray & McNaughton, 2010). Many SMEs owner managers, prior to setting up their own business, had necessary working experiences in the area of their interest. These experiences could have strengthened the core competencies of the SMEs owner managers, and thus reduced the learning curve for a number of aspects of the business (Marc, 2001). In the qualitative study, three respondents acknowledged this factor, and 79% of the respondents from the quantitative study (50%, to large extent; 28.9%, to very large extent). The result showed significant influence of this factor to the decision making process. As suggested by Richard (2013), SMEs owner managers are in better position towards success if they have built up competitive advantages through their past experiences, and these experiences will definitely help them in managing their business. However, there have also been conflicting studies that have reported weak or inconsistent support for experience as an important factor in the decision making process (Sousa, Ruzo & Losada, 2010). Moreover, there is also limited number of works on the effect of experience on decision making process. Within the context of this present research, the results of the data analysis confirm that past experience is one of the influential factors in the decision making process.

From the quantitative survey, it was found that financial return was the most influential factor in the decision making process perceived by the respondents (86%). In any business environment, a decision maker may intentionally prioritise financial return above any reasons. This factor, as cited in many studies, is important in any type of organisations (Uma and Bhuvanes, 2011), and is the main motivator for the growth of SMEs. For the SMEs decision makers, the perceived benefit (in terms of profit) needs to outweigh the anticipated risk in marketing for a positive decision to be made. There is considerable support in SME literature for financial return as one of the relevant factors concerning the decision making process (Barcellos, Cyrino, Junior & Fleury, 2010) Moreover, most of the respondents in the qualitative survey also agreed that financial return or profit margin is always the top priority in the marketing process. As reinforced by Uma and Bhuvanes (2011), SMEs are not always interested in marketing unless there is a need for growth/ expansion, or profits.

In most cases, SMEs' financial capability is the most critical factor that requires the SMEs owner managers to be cautious of their investment and spending (Tamara, 2010; Ghobakhloo, 2011). However, in some research, the costs of marketing are defined as implicitly hidden because the costs or expenses are low (Gilmore *et al.*, 2001). For example, the costs of marketing include minor expenses such as dinner and entrance fees to exhibitions. Therefore, SMEs owner managers do not consciously need to consider these costs. This argument is however not in line with the current research where more than 71% of the respondent in the quantitative study and two respondents in the qualitative study (Company B and Company C) acknowledged the importance of this factor, thus supporting Tamara (2010) and Ghobakhloo (2011).

Market size is one of the determinants in decision making process by SMEs (Jocumsen, 20012). Previous research has shown that the greater is the market opportunity, the more are the SMEs increasingly becoming committed in their investments (Deng, 2003). Market size refers to the potential growth of the target market, and is used as an indicator of the commitment from SMEs in their decision (Deng, 2003; McDonal, 2010). However, the commitment of SMEs to growth is mainly restricted by physical resources (Nor Hazlina & Pi, 2009), which also exhibits their marketing characteristics (Joensuu, 2009). Likewise, SMEs are found to operate with a small number of customers, thus they are able to respond quickly on any problems and queries (Carson, 1993). In this study, the decision maker from the Company C highlighted the importance this factor as evidenced from his quote, "...*China is one of the good places to start as we face fierce competition locally.*..." This finding perhaps explains the reason for the market size not being a significant indicator that influences the marketing decision making process.

Risk, a familiar concept in SME business, was quoted by all the respondents in the qualitative study. The result in the quantitative study further showed that 86% of the respondents acknowledged the importance of this factor in influencing their decision making process. Risk taking has long been associated with the SMEs business nature that takes social, psychological, and financial risks to create something new, and to achieve independence and financial rewards. Risk taking has also been empirically documented to be having influence on decision outcome (Naldi *et al.*, 2007; Lee, 2012; Richard, 2013). Sousa, Ruzo & Losada (2010) have found that SMEs decision makers who were risk takers were more likely to succeed in their venture. Risk impact in this study was found in the coefficient analysis that showed significant influence and negative relationship with decision outcome. This finding supports the studies of Naldi, Nordqvist, Sjöberg, & Wiklund (2007) that suggests a negative relationship between risk taking behaviour and decision outcome. This means that SMEs decision makers in quantitative study took lesser risk in their consideration throughout the decision making process. However, this finding contradicts with other study that suggests risk is positively associated with decision outcome (Rauch, Wiklund, Frese, & Lumpkin, 2004; Karla Díaz, Ute Rietdorf, & Utz Dornberger, 2011). This evident in the qualitative survey where some of the respondents demonstrated high level perception on both risk and the outcome which supported positive relationship. In this regards, explanation on risk impact to the decision outcome can be concluded as a subject to the understanding of the decision maker himself (Lee, 2012).

The size of SMEs is somehow important in reflecting the firms' capability to absorb the cost, which is critical for SMEs. The size of the company also reflects the characters of SME marketing. When companies are being financially sound or successful, the size of the company may affect their willingness to spend in marketing activity, which is a subject to the level of risk. Therefore, SMEs might use scare resources in order to legitimate or lessen the financial risk, and apply control-based approach that is critically associated with cost advantage (Oliver Gassmann & Peter Hürzeler, 2013). Moreover, the findings in this study are consistent with the finding of Ji Junzhe (2010) that firm size is important for international entry mode decision. However, the findings in the qualitative study revealed that only Company B acknowledged this factor as evidenced in the following quote: "...*size of company is unlikely to allow us to expand the business overnight.*" This finding is supported by the finding in quantitative study as only 14% of the respondents acknowledged the importance of this factor in influencing the decision making process among the SMEs.

6.1.2 Discussion on "Do these factors (driving factors) significantly influence the decision outcome?

Based on result in the qualitative study, factors such as personal competency, profit margin, and risk size were acknowledged by all the respondents as important in their decision making process. This finding was also confirmed in the quantitative study as these factors were found to be at the top three factors perceived as important by the respondents. Further analysis using multiple regressions suggested significant relationship between the driving factors and decision outcome. This means that increased level of involvement of these factors in the decision making process tends to improve the decision outcome. The findings provide empirical evidence to support the notion that the driving factors are significant contributors to performance of SME decision making process, eventually leading to growth and profitability (Covin & Miles, 1999; Covin & Wales, 2011). One null hypothesis (Ho1) in relation to this research question was constructed to examine the influence of the driving factors to the decision outcome. The result thus revealed that the null hypothesis was accepted.

In this study, 12 driving factors namely personal vision, personal competency, long-term business relationship, goal setting, personal and lifestyle consideration, ethical and social consideration, personal experience, financial return, company financial capability, market size, risk size, and size of company were evaluated to identify the influence on the adoption of decision making method used by the SMEs owner managers. Result from the analysis revealed that these variables significantly predicted the decision outcome. The result also revealed that financial return (profit margin) was the strongest influence to the decision outcome. The influence of financial return to the quality of decision outcome has extensively been discussed in previous researches (e.g., Uma & Bhuvanes, 2011; Barcellos, Cyrino, Junior & Fleury, 2010). Undoubtedly, financial return is the important instrument that determines the most appropriate decision making process in order to achieve a good and effective decision (Elliot, 1998).

6.2 Discussion on Research Question 2

6.2.1 Discussion on "What are the sources of information considered in making a decision for marketing?"

To achieve a good, SMEs need to seek information from the business environment (Varis & Littunen, 2010). This notion is supported by the studies carried out by Keh et al. (2007) and Cacciolatti et al. (2011). According to them, the good use of information by the organisation can lead to a higher probability of growth, and enhance the competitiveness as well as a better decision making process (M. Krishna Moorthy, Annie, Carolineoo, Chang Sue Wei, Jonathan Tan Yong Ping, and Tan Kah Leong, 2012). In this study, 15 information sources were identified, namely past experience, formal education, other business managers (similar business, competitors), friends/ social networks, suppliers, customers, family, media (including TV, newspapers, and magazines, etc), the Internet, external private sector consultants (banker, accountant, lawyer), banks or other financial institutions, seminars/conference/ workshops, marketing/trade exhibition, industry or SMEs associations, and Government (SME Corp., Matrade, etc). These sources were commonly used by the respondents in both surveys.

The result showed that the most important source of information used by the SMEs owner managers in both surveys was past experience. This finding was consistent with the previous literature that revealed SMEs marketing is largely done through networking (Gilmore *et al.*, 2001) or combination between relationship and network marketing (Brodie, 1997). Thus, the findings of previous studies tend to associate SMEs marketing with the networking elements such as customers, suppliers (Young, 1999; Pineda, 1997; 2003), friends or social networks, other owner managers, and families (Elaine *et al.*, 2007) as the sources of business information for SME. This finding was probably the reason SMEs owner managers preferred to start the business in an area in which they thought comfortable and have competitive advantage, thus they can use their experience in managing the business. It has also been concluded by Kakkonen (2005) and Stephane (2010) that SMEs decision makers with high levels of experience are often successful in their decisions. Indeed, decision makers with more experience make different decision making process from those with no experience (Fabio Musso, Barbara & Francioni, 2012). Finally, according to Nielsen and Nielsen (2011), decision makers are often influenced by prior knowledge and experiences, which help develop superior ability for the decision makers to manage their decision making process as well as to adopt the decision outcome (Musso & Francioni, 2012).

Customers, as discussed in previous literature, are considered the most important source in providing information to the SMEs owner managers (Newton, 2001; Rafee, 1994). However, in this research, customers were ranked in both surveys as the second most important source of information after past experience. This finding is in concurrence with the finding of Elaine (2007) who found that SMEs owner managers have reduced their dependency on information given by customers in the process of making the decision. In other words, SMEs owner managers have changed their decision dependency. It was however noticed that SMEs owner managers who were close with their customers would gain competitive advantage in terms of differentiating and positioning their product or services. This finding has been highlighted by Elaine (2007) who states that organisational nature of SMEs permits them to concentrate and focus on the relationship with their customers.

Next, friends and social networks were ranked as equally important as customers in this study. This result contradicted with previous studies that ranked customers, suppliers, and other owner managers as the most and useful sources of information (Rafi, 1994; Newton, 2001). The emergence of friends and social networks as among the importance sources of information was probably driven by the introduction of new communication technologies such as Facebook, twitter, e-mail, SMS, IM, and Skype, which have potentially improved SMEs communication (Syed & Nilufar, 2007).

The communication through these media has been observed to be effective (Elaine, 2007) as the owner managers could exchange and share information fast and at any time. The change in the current society towards the use of IT may explain some of the findings that were different from the previous studies.

Elaine (2007) in her study found that other business managers as equally important and useful as the customers in providing right information to influence the decision making process among SMEs owner managers. However, in this study, the importance of this resource was placed after friends and social networks. This finding supports the earlier finding that the introduction of new communication technology provides SMEs owner managers with wider choice of information sources in their decision making process. This finding also explains the reason suppliers and families were ranked less important, unlike as reported by previous studies, e.g., Beatty and Talpade (1994) and Suraj (2001). This present study demonstrated that SMEs decision makers can exploit positive benefits from other business managers more effectively than their family, thus may explain why family as a source of information is getting less important (Manuel Eberhard, 2013)

In this study, the importance of media, the Internet, and seminars/conference/workshops were equally ranked at 21.4% by the respondents. The results for media and the Internet in managing their businesses were somehow correspondent with the adoption rate in Malaysia, which stood at only 30% of total SME establishment (Lim, 2005) despite the extensive use by the SMEs in developing country (Newton, 2001). However, it was argued that information from the Internet has become a common practice (Cunningham et al., 2002) as it is accessible in many instances (Lawrence, 2010). This finding also suggests that the Internet helps the decision makers in processing and analysing information as well as in assessing their ability to penetrate the market (Shane, 2013). The ability to utilise technology and information systems is the key influence of the competitiveness of SMEs as most of them hindered from growth and efficient functioning by the inability to use information technology effectively (Kamal *et al.*, 2011; Celina, 2012). The dramatic increase in the use of the Internet for business functions has also created its own set of technological, educational, and business strategy problems (Craig, 2013). Moreover, the low adoption of information from seminars/conference/workshops in this study concurs the finding of Elaine (2007) who reports that owner managers found that the information from seminars/conference/workshops is limitedly helpful, and these owner managers rarely rely on formal training. SMEs typically spend modestly on marketing expenditures, and utilise few of the available marketing techniques, as many of SMEs decision makers prefer to rely on previous experience and common sense (Tamara, 2012). In this present study, the finding indicated that the information from the seminars/conference/workshops was not usually used by the SMEs owner managers in their business after they returned from the seminars/conference/workshops.

External private consultant, financial institutions, and Government were ranked as the three least used sources of information in providing information to the process of marketing decision. This finding concurs with Newton (2001) and Elaine (2007). SMEs owner managers often perform multifunctional roles in the company, thus they exert strong influences over all aspects of the business including areas that they have no expertise. This approach very often comes to end with exhausted and frustrated owner managers and businesses that are not able to function due to lack of professional input (Richard, 2007).

In this study, exhibitions such as SME Innovation Showcase, SME Convention, and Malaysia International Halal Showcase were ranked as equally important with suppliers as a source of information. This finding contradicts with the report by Elaine (2007) that suggests SMEs in United Stated of America (USA) acquire limited information or benefit from the trade exhibitions conducted by the United Stated of America (USA) Government. In contrary, the Government of Malaysia acknowledges that SME marketing capabilities remain a weak point for their development. Hence, aforementioned programme has been carefully implemented to support SMEs to improve their marketing process. The encouragement and support from the Government are perhaps the reasons for SMEs in Malaysia using information obtained from exhibitions more frequently than other countries.

In the study by Newton (2001), SME association was ranked higher than the Internet. Such a finding is consistent with the finding in this present study. In Malaysian context, the influence of SME association concentrated according to ethnic identities. There are three major ethnicities in the country, namely Malay, Chinese, and Indian. Among those ethnicities, the Chinese has been controlling most of major sectors in Malaysia since the British legacy (Syahira, 2009). Likewise, Chinese business associations are more active in providing business information and support to their members than other ethnicities. These associations significantly provide important information, consultation, and guidance to SMEs owner managers to pursue their business.

Many studies in SME have recognised the importance of managerial characteristics such as education in influencing the decision making process (Musso & Francioni, 2012). It has been suggested that education influences the belief structure of decision makers (Perk, 2009) by specifically increasing management knowledge, competence, and confidence (Lau, 2011), which are significant influencers of attitude. However, past research on the effect of education on mode change has received inconsistent empirical support with pros as many as cons. Within the context of the present research, the results of the data analysis were quite conclusive and not particularly surprising to the researcher. The findings are in line with the results of previous investigation, e.g., by Lau (2011) that suggests positive relationship between decision makers' education level and their decision making process (Musso & Francioni, 2012).

6.2.2 Discussion on "Are there any significant differences in adoption on sources of information based on the decision maker's characteristic (gender, age, ethnicity, and education level)"

As discussed in the literature, SMEs owner managers play a crucial role in the marketing process as they have more direct effect on the decision making process than the CEO of a large corporation (Payne *et al.*, 2005). SMEs owner managers are often the seekers and assimilators of information (Lybaert, 1998) although they may not necessarily recognise the need for it (Fuelhart & Glasmeier, 2003). As the influences of SMEs owner managers appear to be significant in this process, the characteristics of SMEs owner managers undoubtedly influence the adoption of source of information (Leepaibon, 2007). This section deals with the demographics of the respondents including their gender, age, ethnicity, and education level in relation to the four null hypotheses on differences in adoption of source of information among the decision makers. All the hypotheses were accepted and have been summarised in Table 6.1.

The results in this study revealed that 100% of the respondents in the qualitative survey and 85.7% of the respondents in the quantitative survey were male. Only 14.3% of the respondents in the quantitative survey were females. These results were not considered as a gender bias. Instead, mixed samples between males and females were the ultimate goal in this research. As a result, the null hypothesis Ho2 was constructed, and further T-test was needed. Result from the test of the null hypothesis Ho2 revealed that gender factor did affect the differences in source of information in marketing decision making process. The results show that female decision maker tends to be more resources in adoption of information than male decision maker. The findings of this study reinforce previous studies that female decision maker tend to be more willing to take risks, and appear to be more innovative and proactive that leads to increase performance (Ahl, 2006; Zimmerman & Brouthers, 2012: Rosli &

Norshafizah, 2013). This suggests that female decision maker may survive the dynamic, fast- faced and complex business environment which is characterized by shorter life cycles, globalization, and continuous improvements in technology.

With respect to age, the ages below 40 years old accounted 50% of the sampled population, indicating half of the respondents involved in this study were young entrepreneurs. The remaining 50% of the sample were respondents between 40 and 55 years old. This result indicated that the SMEs owner managers had gained necessary working experiences before setting up their own business (Rocha, de Mello, Pacheco, de Abreu Farias, 2012; Nielsen & Nielsen, 2010; Gray & McNaughton, 2010), which then influenced the way they adopted the information. Moreover, from the result, it can also be concluded that the older SMEs owner managers were more resourceful in finding the information (Heck *et al.*, 1995) as they had established personal contact and networking in their previous work experience.

In terms of ethnic groups, the largest group of the respondents identified themselves as Malay (57.1%), followed by Chinese (28.6%) and Indian (14.3%). This finding was somehow contradictory with the actual business scenario where, in 2008, the Chinese ethnic controlled 42% of business ownership, while the Malay ethnic controlled 15% of business ownership (mid-term review of the Malaysia Ninth Plan, 2010). The low response from the Chinese ethnic was expected due to sceptical perception among them towards other ethnics particularly in sharing their business information. In contrary, the high number of Malay respondents was mainly because they were comfortable to be approached by a Malay researcher. The key issue highlighted here is that the ethnics operate within each group's contact and domain, which then could influence the way they approach the decision making process (Shahira, 2009). Furthermore, inferential analysis (ANOVA) to test the null hypothesis Ho5 revealed that the ethnicity factor did affect the adoption of source of information among the SMEs decision makers in this study. Unarguably, these three broad ethnic groups namely Malay, Chinese, and Indian showed differences in adoption of source of information resulting from the imbalance in business ownership (Donald, 2010).

With regards to education level, majority of the respondents in the qualitative study indicated that they received some types of formal education (MBA) before setting up their business. The finding is similar with the quantitative study where more than 64% of the respondents either had a bachelor's degree or a Master's degree. Fabio (2012) suggests that decision makers with high level of education have more possibilities to develop more rational and formal decision making process. This finding is however contradictory with the finding by Knowles and White (1995) who state that many entrepreneurs leave school at an early age to pursue their business interests. As business owners with higher education are more likely to manage business with greater growth potential, it is possible that they are more structured in the process of making decision. Results of the test of the null hypothesis Ho6 indicated that there was a significant difference in adoption of source of information among different levels of education. This finding means that the level of education may be a determining factor in the adoption of source of information (Elaine, 2007; Richard, 2013).

Table 6.1: Summary of the Results of the Null Hypotheses (Research Question 2)

Hypothesis	Description	Result
Ho2	*There is a significant difference among the genders of SMEs decision makers in adoption of source of information.*	Accepted
Ho3	*There is a significant difference among the ages of SMEs decision makers in adoption of source of information.*	Accepted

Ho4	*There is a significant difference among the ethnicities of SMEs decision makers in the adoption of source of information.*	Accepted
Ho5	*There is a significant difference among the education levels of SMEs decision makers in the adoption of source of information.*	Accepted

6.3 Discussion on Research Question 3

6.3.1 Discussion on "What is the decision making method used in making marketing decision? Are there any significant differences in the adoption of decision method based on the decision maker's characteristic (gender, age, ethnicity, and education level)"

There are some similarities and contrasts of opinion between the respondents from the qualitative and quantitative surveys concerning the method of making marketing decision. In the qualitative survey, three decision making methods were indicated by the respondents, which were formal, informal, and combination of both formal and informal methods. Company A reportedly had used informal method in the information gathering process mainly through established networking circle. A simple financial analysis was used to justify for "go or no go" decision. Meanwhile, both Company B and C reportedly used combination of formal and informal methods in different types of business. This mixed method had effectively led throughout their decision making process. Both decision makers were MBA graduates who had received proper marketing skills and knowledge from their formal education. They reportedly used a formal assessment to gather and analyse information from different sources. The analysis was then used as a part of the decision making process. Moreover, in the process, they also consulted established networking as a part of their formal assessment process. The decision maker from Company D was also an MBA graduate, who was a marketing expert with high experience in dealing with the top decision makers in government sector. In this organisation, a highly structured, formalised decision making process was undertaken with some key stakeholder consultation included. Although more structured approach was reported in Company B, C, and D, the informal element was still present in every decision particularly in information gathering, which was evident through the change in the process to match the preferred outcomes. With no doubt, this is the reality of small firm's marketing practice, which is informal, intuitive, and selling-focused (Ondřej Zach, 2012). SMEs are likely to be adaptable (Metts, 2011) to implementing new initiatives as they are less likely to be "locked-in" to their existing processes. SMEs, which are characterised by limited resources, high missing information, and decision uncertainty, seem reasonable in simplifying the decision making process. On the other hand, the need to react quickly in SMEs causes most of the activities to be governed by informal rules and procedures, with low degree of standardisation and formalisation.

On the other hand, from quantitative survey, four methods were indicated to be practised by the respondents, which were formal, informal, combination of both formal and informal methods, and strategic marketing decision. There was similarity in both surveys where informal approach was the common approach among the SMEs decision makers (36%, informal; 36%, combination of formal and informal). This finding supported the finding in the qualitative survey that decision making method in SME environment was largely driven by the informal process (Eliene, 2007; Kieren, 2009; Joensuu, 2009; Marwan, 2010). Implementation of marketing principles is a problematic to most SMEs, which is evident in some specific weaknesses with respect to pricing, planning, training, and forecasting. Many researchers such as Stokes (1994), Gilmore, Carson and Grant (2001), and Tamara (2012) state that evidence of marketing practice, as prescribed in the textbooks, is rarely found in small firms. SMEs owner managers in practice are more generalists rather than specialists. In order words, as according to Tamara (2010), "Formal marketing approach may be interesting to the SME decision maker but it is unlikely to relate closely enough to their specific requirements or to solve the company problems." Marketing process within the SME is much related to the SMEs owner managers' characteristics such as their experience and knowledge in marketing. SMEs decision makers have little time to think strategically about the marketing, and do not believe that formal marketing process will benefit their business, even though balance between formal and informal planning often produces good results (Tamara, 2012). Evidence suggests many successful SMEs do not practise what is conventionally described as strategic approach. Their practice is rather based on the experience, personal knowledge, and intuition towards the people with the key roles in the company (Masoomeh *et al.*, 2011).

Despite conforming previous literature that informal decision is common approach used in most SME, the presence of formal and strategic approaches is also significantly evident in the context of this study as shown by 28% of the respondents (7% indicate formal decision & 21% indicate strategic decision) examined in the quantitative survey. Hence, it can be suggested that, in the context of this study, SME decision making process is no longer totally associated with the image of being informal, unstructured, and spontaneous (Gilmore *et al.*, 2001). Instead, some of the SMEs decision makers implemented structured and strategic decision making process. The most common view is that SMEs prefer simple marketing process that consequently limits their characteristics. This view has now being been challenged with the finding that SMEs do practise strategic decision making (Jocumsen, 2002; Tamara, 2012). It can be argued here that managerial decision characteristics in any types of organisation are not restricted to one type of classification, i.e., either structured, routine, and unstructured, as stated by Marwan *et al.* (2010). Instead, in this study, it was found that the SMEs owner managers could adopt different approaches in meeting their needs. This finding indicated an acceptance among

Hairul Rizad and Abu Bakar

SMEs decision makers towards formal and strategic approaches, and transition from the previous state through improvement in knowledge/education, competency development, and training (Masoomeh *et al.*, 2011). This finding indicates that the present SMEs decision makers have been more educated and knowledgeable and attended development programme. From the qualitative survey, the result showed 3 out 4 the decision makers interviewed possessed an MBA degree. This finding suggests that more and more SMEs decision makers acknowledge the benefit of formal and strategic approaches in helping them improve their competitiveness. This claim is supported by the empirical evidence that suggests that there is a relationship between strategic approach and SME survival and success (Kraus, *et al.*, 2008; Tamara, 2012).

6.3.2 Discussion on "Are there any significant differences in adoption on sources of information based on the decision maker's characteristic (gender, age, ethnicity, and education level)?"

Many studies in SME marketing have recognised the importance of decision makers' characteristics in improving management knowledge, competence, and confidence (Lau, 2011), and this area of study has been well-documented (Perk, 2009; Lau, 2011; Sousa, Ruzo & Losada, 2010; Richard, 2013). According to Tamino (2013), SMEs decision makers' characteristics are regarded as highly relevant for the firms' decision making process. This notion is based on the argument that the SMEs decision makers are often the owners who have the ultimate power of control, and who commonly oversee every aspect of the business. Often they are the only ones with the responsibility and access to the information needed in the decision making process. Within the context of this research, the results of the data analysis were quite conclusive and not particularly surprising to this researcher. From the ANOVA analysis, it was evident that the decision makers' characteristics such as gender, age, ethnicity, and education level significantly affected the adoption of decision making method. This finding was supported by the result of the hypotheses developed, as shown in Table 6.2.

Table 6.2: Summary for the Result of the Null Hypotheses (Research Question 3)

Hypothesis	Description	Result
Ho6	*There is a significant difference among the genders of SMEs decision makers in adoption of decision method.*	Accepted
Ho7	*There is a significant difference among the ages of SMEs decision makers in adoption of decision method.*	Accepted
Ho8	*There is a significant difference among the ethnicities of SMEs decision makers in the adoption of decision method.*	Accepted
Ho9	*There is a significant difference among the education levels of SMEs decision makers in the adoption of decision method.*	Accepted

6.4 Research Question 4

6.4.1 Discussion on "Are there any significant relationships between the adoption of decision making method and the decision outcome?"

In the qualitative study, all the respondents expressed satisfaction on the outcome of the decision making process. This was evident in the following quote from Company D : *"I'm satisfied with the process and the quality of information collected from various sources. It's regarded as a success and I keep reviewing it for improvement."* This finding was supported the ANOVA analysis that revealed a positive relationship between decision making method and decision outcome, thus supporting the hypothesis.

Table 6.3: Summary for the Result of the Null
Hypotheses (Research question 4)

No.	Hypothesis	Result
Ho10	*There is a relationship between the decision method used in the decision making process and the decision outcome.*	Accepted

6.5 Discussion on model of marketing decision making process for SMEs

Based on the findings discussed in this chapter, a model of SMEs marketing decision making process was developed, as illustrated in Figure 6.1. This model was tested using inferential analysis to provide understanding on how marketing decision making process was implemented by SMEs. The process included decision makers' characteristics, sources of information, driving factors, and decision outcome.

Figure 6.1: A model of SMEs marketing decision making process

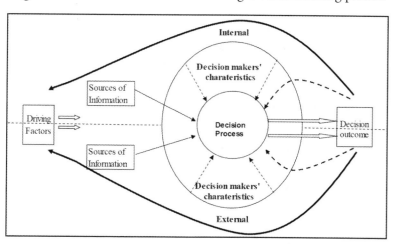

Decision makers' characteristics, in this study, were found to be significant in influencing the adoption of sources of information and the adoption of decision making method during decision making process. As discussed in previous section, the SMEs owner mangers tended to choose the type of business that they had working experience in and operated based on their personal experiences, values, and personal characteristics-all these then determined the future survivability of their organisations. For example, an owner-founder was more likely to start a new venture in an industry familiar to him than venturing into an unfamiliar marketplace with no established business relationships. As a result, his decisions were different from the manager in large organisation. This finding extends the findings of several other studies related to influence of decision makers' characteristics (e.g., Uma & Bhuvanes, 2011; Syahira, 2009; Elaine, 2007) on marketing decision making process.

Identifying information relevant to the decision is a critical first step. If the relevant information is incorrectly identified, or if any critical elements are missing, the analysis of the information will be inherently flawed. Thus, the analysis built on a faulty foundation could lead to an ineffective decision. After the information needed to make the decision has been identified, the SMEs decision makers must gather the information. Forbes (2005) states that the process of assembling information is as heterogeneous as the SMEs decision makers themselves. Information is collected from different sources, and the degree to which information comes from each source depends upon the situation. Assembling the information assists the SMEs decision makers to reduce the gap between what is known and what is not known. SMEs typically do not have functional employees within their company (Pineda *et al.*, 1998), so the SMEs owner managers, who generally are decision makers, are responsible for assembling the necessary information regardless of the departments of the company.

According to Stephanie (2010), the extent of information seeking by the decision makers is directly related to the level of importance of the decision. For complex decision, SMEs owner managers will gather more information before making the decision. This follows the logics that more important decisions require more careful consideration (Chell & Baines, 2000). In this present study, 15 sources of information were identified as having statistically positive relationship with the adoption of the decision making method. In current business environment, SMEs decision makers face continuous challenges in managing their businesses (Christman, 2005; Mulligan, 2004). These challenges require the decision makers to continuously improve the way of finding the sources of information that is directed to meeting their specific needs (Christman et al., 2005).

When the defined information has been assembled, the next step is to integrate the information into a decision. Each alternative and its attributes are analysed and compared, so that the information gathered in the previous steps forms the foundation for the decision. When evaluating the alternatives, the values assigned to the attributes can be affected by other factors. These factors may be from internal or external. These factors are subject to the perceptions of how the SMEs owner managers perceive the factors affecting the final decision. 12 driving factors, which were statistically significant in influencing the adoption of decision outcome, were identified in this study. These driving factors did not necessarily have a direct influence on the outcomes of decisions, but they may instead act on the information fed into the process.

As discussed in this chapter, no common method is accepted in SMEs environment even though it is largely associated with informal process. This implies the flexibility to SMEs owner managers in understanding the issue, and in applying the appropriate method depending on the complexity of each stage.

In this study, decision outcome was found to have a positive relationship with the adoption of decision making process by the decision makers. According to Libby et al. (1995), decision outcome depends upon the decision making process used. A good decision making process results in good decision. This study also reveals a relationship between driving factor to the outcome of the decision.

6.6   Research Implications

In undertaking this research based on the abovementioned model, the theoretical, methodological, and practical implications have emerged as important considerations for conducting further research on marketing decision making process. The framework for the study and questionnaire design have particular implications for those who wish to do further research in areas involving marketing decision making process from other country's point of view.

6.6.1   Theoretical Implications

This thesis contributes to the SME literature and improves our understanding of the role of decision makers in the decision making process. This study constitutes and offers a complete framework that integrates SMEs decision makers' characteristics and their interaction with sources of information and driving factors that statistically influence the decision making process in making marketing decision. The inclusion of SMEs decision makers' characteristics addresses the limitations that have been largely ignored by prior literature that only stresses on the effect of firm characteristic and networking relationship. The addition of these process elements into the model enriches our understanding of the complexity of SME marketing decision. That is, beside the impacts of aforementioned factors, decision makers can also partially explain variation of the marketing decision making process. This study has brought a certain degree of practicality through addressing the role of decision makers' characteristics in marketing decision making process. This study also essentially moves forward the current model and decision making model, and also increases content-oriented research on SME marketing study.

Moreover, there are four implications of this sequentially mixed method. First, to the best of the researcher's knowledge, there is apparently a lack of research in the context of Malaysia that investigates the process of making marketing decision among SMEs. Second, the impact of decision makers' characteristics on the decision making process in supporting the current research (e.g., Perk, 2009; Lau, 2011; Sousa, Ruzo & Losada, 2010; Richard, 2013; Tamino, 2013) plays an important role in determining a process, as well as the perception of the situation. Third, different from the past studies, the role of driving factor in this study is recognised as a medium in selecting and analysing the information. Finally, the study includes and statistically examines the impact of decision makers' characteristics on marketing decision making process. Decision makers' characteristics such as age, gender, ethnicity, and education level were found to be significantly affecting the justification of sources of information and adoption of decision making process. This finding suggests that academics should be aware of decision making process elements in terms of the involvement of sources of information, and driving factors and interaction of these elements in producing the decision outcome.

Besides, this thesis makes a contribution to the SME literature by providing an exploratory theory model that improves our understanding on the process of making marketing decision in SME. The model developed in this study reveals that although decision makers' characteristics appear to be the key drivers of competitive advantage, the interactions among the sources of information and driving factors are also crucial in improving the outcome.

This research also has implications in questionnaire design. In this research, the survey questionnaire was designed based on the findings from the prior qualitative survey, from which highly useful information was gathered. Questionnaires used in previous studies were narrowed down in scope as they only focused on a limited number of stages, thus findings from these studies were unable to fully ascertain SMEs decision makers' behaviour. In contrast, by using the fieldwork result as the basis for designing the questionnaires, the results were able to yield more practical understanding on decision makers' needs in making marketing decision making process. Therefore, the questionnaire developed from the result of Phase 1 provides a wide understanding of the factors affecting SMEs in marketing decision making process. In addition, the questionnaire designed in this present study can be also analysed using both combination of descriptive and inferential analyses.

Based on the combination of theories (details are in Chapter 2), this research has found that: (1) the theories can be used to establish a complete model for SMEs marketing decision making in Malaysia; and (2) the theories provide a strong basis for improving marketing skills in the process of making marketing decision. The model developed in this study contains three parts including decision makers' characteristics, factors affecting the adoption of decision making method, and decision outcome. Other than that, in terms of implications in the use of this model, researchers undertaking similar studies should undertake holistic approach suggested by this model rather than opting for piecemeal approach that is very commonly used. In adopting the holistic approach outlined in this model, the comprehensive questionnaire used in the survey is able to establish a good understanding of the complex issues involved in SMEs marketing decision making process.

6.6.2 Methodology implication

The methodology used in this study can provide guidelines for similar researches in future, including recruitment of suitable respondents, and questionnaire design and presentation. Among the guidelines are as follows: (1) Because the survey is distributed using email addresses extracted from SMEs listing, the follow-up approach using email is not suitable as the respondents might not open their email regularly. Hence, it is advised for direct follow-up through phone calls rather than reminder through emails; and (2) The mixed method used in this research is suitable for exploratory research where the qualitative research finding can also be used as a guideline to construct the quantitative survey instrument.

6.6.3 Practical Implications

In terms of practical implications, the model presented in Figure 6.1 can be used in understanding organisational conditions that must be present in order to achieve a desirable outcome. This will encourage decision makers to identify the suitable sources of information to facilitate the process of evaluation. The framework will also help decision makers identify the driving factors that can contribute positive outcome.

The Malay trade associations such as the Malay Chamber of Commerce (DPMM) and the Malaysian Business and Industrial Association (PERDASAMA) must play their effective role in promoting the SMEs development and the competitiveness of their members than just being active pressure groups. They have to explore the possibilities on how to they can assist their members to be more competitive in the open market rather than being dependent on government contracts and licenses. They must also make themselves a focal point for SMEs to seek guidance and assistance in entrepreneurial matters.

Moreover, this study found that entrepreneurship is yet to be seen as a career of choice by SMEs owner managers. This is due to the lack of an entrepreneurship culture that has eventually contributed to their lack of entrepreneurial development. Therefore, efforts should be undertaken by the Government to promote entrepreneurship as a career option as well as to inculcate entrepreneurship culture among the Malaysians through exposing them to the entrepreneurship activities and knowledge at an early age in the country's education system. In this regard, entrepreneurship study should be made part of the school curriculum, from kindergarten to secondary level, instead of only being extra-curricular activities like the present practice. The current education should also be aggressively reviewed in order to promote independent learning, skills development, and creative thinking among the Malaysian children as these elements are essential for their entrepreneurial development.

6.7   Limitations of the Study

The previous section discusses the potential contributions that this thesis had made to the extant literature and knowledge. However, like other studies, this research also has several limitations.

First, despite the benefits of mixed methods used by the researchers, this approach is a challenge in that it requires more work and financial resources, and takes more time than singular methods (Molina-Azorín, 2011). The practical difficulties to a large extent limited the current research in terms of sample planning. As have been noted in Chapter Three, there are some gaps in qualitative and quantitative sampling. The qualitative data were collected from interview with four SMEs decision makers who were mainly from Transport and Trading sector. However, the quantitative data covered wider sectors including Automotive, Building & Construction, Electric & Electronics, Manufacturing, Trading, and Transport. As a result, the result of qualitative study that was mainly from two sectors were generalised to develop quantitative instrument. In addition, because of the problems with access to targeted interviewees, the approached interviewees depended largely on the participants' willingness to help, and thus may not achieve the purpose of maximum variation.

Second, for the qualitative component of this study, the fact that the research topic involved sensitive information not only made it difficult to get access to the targeted interviewees, but also made the participants very cautious about providing detailed and in-depth information. Some interviewees were anxious about confidentiality. Some parts of the conversation were requested no to recorded by the interviewees. Although actions were taken in dealing with this problem, such as writing down whatever the researcher remembered as soon as possible after each interview, some points were still lost in such a situation. This may reduce the reliability of the qualitative study.

Third, the qualitative part of this thesis shared some common problems with other qualitative researches. Prior literature argues that qualitative research may have potential bias imposed by the researcher in the processes of conducting interviews and analysing data (McKinnon, 1988; Bryman, 2004). The researcher in the current study recognised that this study is not free from subjectivity and bias that may influence the research processes, such as sample selection, formulation of interview questions, and data coding. In order to reduce the bias, the researcher tried to be as thorough and consistent as possible at the stages of data collection and data analysis. For example, interviews were carefully transcribed, and the transcripts or notes were checked with interviewees so as to ensure that the collected raw data were unbiased and represented the interviewees' views accurately. Moreover, data were coded following a consistent and systematic coding procedure, and interpretation was discussed with supervisors.

Finally, it is also acknowledged that the presence of male respondents only in qualitative study can be a question, as this issue can trigger a gender bias. It is therefore noted that the outcome of qualitative study to generalise the instrument development with a significant presence of female population is not really appropriate. The impact of female respondents in the development of quantitative survey of this study, despite males dominating the SME sector, should also be acknowledged.

6.8   Recommendations for Further Research

Previous sections discuss the contribution that this thesis has made, and some limitations that it has. Next, this section outlines several avenues for future research, and concludes this thesis.

This thesis is an exploratory study that investigates the SME marketing decision making process using mixed methods. It sheds the light on how the combination of quantitative and qualitative approaches can better explore the complicated social phenomenon. Mixed methods research has attracted increasing attention in social science studies. Molina-Azorín (2011) examines the prevalence, characteristics, and added value of mixed methods articles published in two management fields, and finds that the prevalence rate of four management journals is lower than those found by other scholars in mathematics education research journals. Given the advantages that mixed methods research can take, more research that combines and integrates quantitative and qualitative methods in different ways should be undertaken in the SME fields.

Specifically, future qualitative research may want to extend the present study in other aspects. In this study, the findings of the qualitative study showed that the decision making process among the respondents was different than in their practice. Some of them appeared to be more advanced than others in implementing the process. This provides an avenue for future research to explore the difference in decision makers' competency in decision making process. Moreover, the qualitative approach of this study focused on the views of SMEs decision makers and their role in the decision making process, particularly on gathering the information and influencing the usage of the information. However, there are many other stakeholders who may also be involved in supplying or influencing the use of information related to the decision making process, such as customers, other business managers, and family members. Therefore, future interview-based research could extend the present study by investigating the perspectives of other groups of participants to understand how they help mediate the SMEs in the process of making marketing decision, besides exploring other contributing factors that may provide necessary support in the process. Such broader perspective could provide more comprehensive picture on the process of SMEs marketing decision.

6.9   Conclusion

This study enriches the SMEs marketing literature by contributing to a deeper understanding of SMEs marketing decision making process in Malaysia. This study provides better understanding on the interaction of SMEs owner managers' personal characteristics in relation to source of information and driving factors for adopting the suitable process in making marketing decision.

The results of this study suggested that SMEs owner managers' personal characteristics (gender, age, ethnicity, and education level) contributed statistically significant to sources of information and driving factors, which then determine the adoption of suitable decision making process. The assumption that SMEs decision making process is mainly informal was found not valid anymore as the SMEs owner mangers also practised structured process in making the decision. This was mainly a contribution from the SMEs owner managers' past experience and education level that had probably increased their competency in making the decision. Additionally, the results also suggested that the outcome of the process was statistically significant to the adoption of decision making process by the decision makers.

Moreover, the results of this study demonstrated that personal competency of the SMEs owner managers had an important role in improving the marketing process. This finding implies that, if we agree that encouraging and nurturing good decision maker is crucial in SMEs development, it is essential for more courses or syllabuses to be included in Malaysian education system with an emphasis on entrepreneurial knowledge, attitude, and skills at all levels.

The deep understanding on SMEs marketing decision making process allows the SMEs owner managers to grow or expand their market reach. To do this, the Government should continue to play a role in developing entrepreneurial and managerial competencies among the SMEs owner managers. Improving and strengthening the SMEs owner managers' competencies will ultimately position them among the catalysts for achieving the vision of Malaysia to become an economically developed country.

In conclusion, the research on SMEs in Malaysia is still in its infancy stage, and there are broad opportunities for further researches. This study is an aperture for other researchers who are interested in delving into this topic further, whether in Malaysian context or in other contexts.

REFERENCES

Abdul Ghani, Yusniza, Apnizan and Syed Zambri (2009), Building Business Networking: A Proposed Framework for Malaysian SMEs, *International Review of Business Research Papers*.Vol.5, pp. 151-160.

Abu Bakar (2003). *A critical analysis of policy initiatives involving small and medium enterprises in Malaysia*. Ph.D. Thesis. Derbyshire business school, University of Derby.

Abdullah, MA 2002, 'Entrepreneurs and their influence on the usage of information technology in SMEs: Evidence from Malaysia', *Journal of Small Business and Entrepreneurship (JSBE)*, vol. 4, No.2. pp. 60-76.

Ali Salman Saleh and Nelson Oly Ndubisi (2006), An Evaluation of SME Development in Malaysia, *International Review of Business Research Papers*. vol.2. pp.1-14.

Alderson (2009). *Exploring The Complexities Of Family Business Decision Making;* PhD. Theses.

Alpkan, L., Yilmaz, C. and Kaya, N. (2007). Market Orientation and Planning Flexibility in SMEs. Performance Implications and an Empirical Investigation. *International Small Business Journal*, 25(2), pp.152-172.

Antonius, R. *Interpreting Quantitative Data with SPSS*, SAGE Publications, London. 2003.

APEC (1994). The APEC Survey on Small and Medium Enterprises.

Appiah-Adu, K. and Singh, S. (1998). Customer orientation and performance. *Management Decision*, 36(6), pp.385-394.

Babbie, E. R. 1990, Survey Research Methods (2nd Edition), Wadsworth Publishing Company, Belmont, California.

Badlisham Ghazali (2012). Malaysia SME ICT Landscape. MOSTI-PIKOM Leadership Summit 2012

Baird (1989). *Managerial decisions under uncertainty: An introduction to the analysis of decision making.* John Wiley and Sons, INC, Toronto.

Bank Negara Malaysia. 2007. Annual Report.

Barnes, J. G. *Secrets of Customer Relationship Management. It's All About How You Make Them Feel.* McGraw-Hill.2001.

Beatty, Sharon and Salil talpade (1994). 'Adolescent influence in Family Decision making: A replication with extension. *Journal of consumer research*, pp. 332- 341.

Bhaskar (2004). Whether to bet, reserve options or insure: Making certain choices in an uncertain world. *Ivey Business Journal.* Vol. 68, pp.1-8.

Blankson, C. & Cheng, J.M-S. (2005). Have small businesses adopted the market orientation concept? The case of small businesses in Michigan. *Journal of Business & Industrial Marketing,* 20(6), pp.317-330.

Blackwell, R. D., Miniard, P. W. and Engel, J. F. *Consumer Behaviour (9th Edition),* Harcourt College Publishers, Florida. 2001.

Buhler (2001). *Managing in the new millennium,* SuperVision.vol.62. pp.13-15.

Brush (2002). The role of social capital and gender in linking financial suppliers and entrepreneurial firms: a framework for future research. *Venture Capital,* 4: pp. 305-323.

Brush, CG, Manolova, TS & Edelman, LF 2008, 'Separated by a Common Language? Entrepreneurship Research Across the Atlantic', *Entrepreneurship: Theory & Practice,* vol. 32, no. 2, pp. 249-66.

Brown, C. (2000). Entrepreneurial education teaching guide. *Digest* 00-7.

Brown, G. W. (2005). 'Developing an Exit Strategy', *RSI Magazine,* February, pp. 22-28.

Busenitz, L., Barney, J. Differences between entrepreneurs and managers in large organizations: Biases and heuristics in strategic decision-making, Journal of Business Venturing, Vol. 12,/1997, pp. 9-30.

Cassell, C, Nadin, S and Gray, MO (2001). The use and effectiveness of benchmarking in SMEs., Benchmarking: *An International Journal,* vol. 8, no. 3, pp. 212-222.

Carson, D. and A. Gilmore (2000), Small Business marketing management competencies, *International Business Review,* 9(3), pp.363-82.

Casson, M.(1991), 'Entrepreneur', *Journal of Economic.*

Chen, Lei (2012) A mixed methods study investigating intangibles in the banking sector. PhD thesis.

Cox, Sarah (2012). "Social Media Marketing in a Small Business: A Case Study". Department of Computer Graphics Technology Degree Theses.

Coviello, N. E., Brodie, R. J. & Munro, H. J. (2000). An Investigation of Marketing Practice by Firm Size. *Journal of Business Venturing,* 15(5/6), pp.523-545.

Cohen, J. (1988). *Statistical Power Analysis for the Behavioral Sciences (2nd Edition),* Lawrence Erlbaum Associates, Hillsdale, N.J.

Culkin, N and Smith, D 2000, 'An emotional business: A guide to understanding the motivations of small business decision takers', *Qualitative Market Research: An International Journal,* vol. 3, no. 3, p. 12.

Crouch, Mira & McKenzie, Heather (2006). The logic of small samples in interview based qualitative research. *Social Science Information,* 45(4), pp. 483-499.

Cyret, R.M., Simon, J.A & Trow, D.B. 1956,'Obervation of business decision', *The Journal of Business,* vol.29, no4, pp.237-248.

Delisle, S & St-Pierre, J 2004, "Decision support for SME owners-managers: a performance evaluation benchmarking tool", in

Decision Support in an Uncertain and Complex World: The IFIP TC8/WG8.3 International Conference, pp. 202-212.

DeVellis, R. F. (2003). Scale Development Theory and Applications (2nd Edition), SAGE Publications, Califomia.

Elaine (2007). *An exploratory study of information resources used by small manufacturing owners in managing their business.* Ph.D. Thesis. Kansas State University.

Einhorn and Hogarth (1981) Behavioral decision theory: Processes of judgment and choice, *Annual Review of Psychology,* vol. 32, pp. 53-58.

Elliott (1998). Experiments in decision making under risk and uncertainty: Thinking outside the box. *Managerial and Decision Economics.* Vol. 19, pp.239-257.

Eisenhardt, K.M and Zbaracki, M.J.1992, Strategic Decision Making. *Strategic management Journal,* vol. 13, pp.17-73.

Eyre, P. and Smallman, C. (1998) Euromanagement Competences in Small and Medium-Sized Enterprises: A Development Path for New Millennium?, *Management Decision,* 36(1), pp.34-42.

Fillis, I. (2002). Small Firm Marketing Theory and Practice: Insights from the Outside. *Journal of Research in Marketing & Entrepreneurship,* 4(2), pp. 134-157.

Fuelhart, K. and Glasmeier, A. (2003). Acquisition, assessment and use of business information by small and medium-sized businesses: a demand perspective. *Entrepreneurship & Regional Development,* 15(3), pp. 229-252.

Feltham, T., Feltham, G., Barnett, J. (2005). The dependence of family businesses on a single decision-maker. *Journal of Small Business Management,* vol. 43(1), pp 1-15

Gibcus P., van Hoesel P. H. Transforming an Idea Into a Strategic Decision in SMEs: the Underlying Decision Making Process, EIM: Zoetermeer, 2004

Gibb, A.A. (1997). Small firms' training and competitiveness: Building upon the small business as a learning organization. *International Small Business Journal.*vol. 15(3), pp. 13-30.

Gibb, A.A. (1993). The enterprise culture and education. *International Small Business Journal.* vol. 11(3), pp. 11-34

Guinevere L. Gilbert(2010). A Sequential Exploratory Mixed Methods Evaluation of Graduate Training and Development in the Construction Industry

Gilmore, A., Carson, D., Grant, K., Pickett, B. and Lancy, R. (2000) 'Managing Strategic Change in Small and Medium-Sized Enterprises: How Do Owner- Managers Hand Over Their Networks?', *Strategic Change* 9(7): pp. 415–426.

Gilmore, A., Carson, D. and Grant, K. (2001), "SME Marketing in Practice", *Marketing Intelligence & Planning*, Vol. 19 No. 1, pp. 6-11.

Goodwin and Wright (1991). *Decision analysis for management judgment.* John Wiley and Sons., Inc, Chichester.

Goodpaster, Kenneth and T. Dean Maines, "US Citizen Bank: A Case Study," Business and Professional Ethics Journal 23:1/2 (Spring/Summer, 2004): pp.93-133.

Goleman, D. 1998. *Emotional Intelligence That Lead to Success, EI 2, pp. 9-42;*

Grieco, D (2007). The Entrepreneurial Decision: Theories, Determinants and Constraints, Liuc Papers, *Economic Journal.*

Gustafsson, V.(2006). *Entrepreneurial Decision-making: Individuals, Tasks and Cognitions*, Cheltenham, UK: Edward Elgar Publishers.

Gomez, E. T., Loh, W. L., and Lee, K. H. (2004). Malaysia. In E. T. Gomez and H. H. Michael Hsiao (Ed.), Chinese Business in Southeast Asia (pp. 62-84). London and New York: RoutledgeCurzon.

Gravetter, F. J. and Wallnau, L. B. (2004). *Statistics for the behavioral sciences (6th Edition),* Wadsworth/Thomson Leaming, Belmont, CA.

Harrison, E.F. and Pelletier, M.A. (2000), 'Levels of strategic decision effectiveness', *Management Decision*, Vol. 38 No. 1/2, pp. 107-118.

Harrison (1999). *The managerial decision making process.* (5th ed.). Houghton Mifflin company, Boston, New York.

Hansson(2005). Decision Theory – A Brief Introduction, 2005, http://www.infra.kth.se/~soh/ decisiontheory.pdf.

Hastie (2001). Problems for judgment and decision making. *Annual Review of Psychology.* vol. 52, pp. 653-83.

Hashim, M. K. (1999). A review of the role of SMEs in the manufacturing sector in Malaysia. *Malaysian Management review,* June: pp.40-49

Hall, H.K., and Kerr, A.W. (2001). Goal setting in sport and physical activity: Tracing empiricaldevelopments and establishing conceptual direction. In G.C. Roberts (Ed.), *Advancesin motivation in sport and exercise* (pp. 183– 234). Champaign, IL: Human Kinetics

Helen Reijonen (2010). Role and practices of marketing in SMEsFaculty of Law, Economics and Business Administration.

Hill, J. and Wright, L.T. (2001), *"A qualitative research agenda for small to medium-sized enterprises"*, Marketing Intelligence & Planning, Vol.19 No. 6, pp. 432-43.

Hudson (2000). Only just managing – no time to measure", in Conference Proceedings Performance Measurement – Past, Present and Future, Cranfield University, Cranfield, pp. 243-250.

Howard, J. A. and Sheth, J. N. 1969, "The Howard-Sheth Theory of Buyer Behaviour" in R. L. Horton (Ed.), Buyer Behaviour: A Decision-Making Approach, Bell and Howell, Ohio, pp.32-36.

Hill, J., McGown, P.(1996). The development and application of a qualitative approach to researching the marketing networks of small firm entrepreneurs. Qualitative Market Research: *An International Journal.* vol 2, pp. 71–81H

Hill, J. (2001). A multidimensional study of the key determinants of effective SME marketing activity: Part 2. *International Journal of Entrepreneurial Behaviour & Research,* 7(6), pp. 211-235.

Hisrich, RD, Peters, MP, Shepherd, DA and Mombourquette, PS (2006). *Entrepreneurship*, McGraw-Hill Ryerson, Toronto, Canada.

Hutu, CA Culture, change, competition, Economic Publishing House, Bucharest, 2003.

Hogarth-Scott, S., Watson, K. & Wilson, N. (1996). Do small businesses have to practice marketing to survive and grow? *Marketing Intelligence & Planning*, 14(1), pp. 6-18.

Hofstede, G. Culture's consequences: International differences in workrelated values, Newbury Park, CA: Sage Publications,

Heck, R., Rowe, B., and Owen, A (1995). Home based employment and Family Life. Wesport, Connecticut:Aubun House

Hester, E. L. 1996, *Successful Marketing Research: The Complete Guide to Getting and Using Essential Information About Your Customers and Competitors*, John Wiley & Sons, Canada.

Indarti, N. and Langenberg, M. 2004. Factors affecting business success among SMEs: Empirical evidences from Indonesia.

Ionescu, Gheorghe Gh Thomas, A. Organizational culture and organizational management, Publishing, Bucharest, 2001.

Jimmy Hills (2001), A multidimensional study of the key determinants of effective SME marketing activity, *International Journal of Entrepreneurial Behaviour & Research*, Vol. 7, No. 6.

Jinhua Shoa (2006). QoS Assessment of Providers with Complex Behaviours: An Expectation-Based Approach with Confidence, Service-Oriented Computing – ICSOC, vol. 4294, 2006, pp 378-389

Jocumsen.G (2004). *"How do small business managers make strategic marketing decisions? A model of process"*, European Journal of Marketing Vol. 38 No. 5/6, 2004 pp. 659-674

Jordan, J.A., & Michel, F.J. (2000). *Next generation manufacturing: methods and techniques*. New York: John Wiley and Sons, Inc.

Helen Reijonen, Role and practice of marketing in SMEs, Theses, University of Joensuu (2009)

Hester, E. L. (1996). *Successful Marketing Research: The Complete Guide to Getting and Using Essential Information About Your Customers and Competitors,* John Wiley & Sons, Canada.

Hudson, M, Lean, J & Smart, PA 2001, "Improving control through effective performance measurement in SMEs", *Production Planning and Control,* vol.12, no. 8, pp. 804-813.

Hague, P. and Jackson, P. 1995, *Do Your Own Market Research (2nd Edition),* Kogan Page, London.

Jocumsen, G.(2004). How do small business managers make strategic marketing decisions? A model of process. *European Journal of Marketing.* vol. 38, pp. 659-674.

Jorosi, B.N. (2006). The information needs and information seeking behaviours of SME managers in Botswana. *Libri,* 56, 97-107

Kieren (2007). *Information Systems Decision Making: Factors Affecting Decision Makers and Outcomes.* Ph.D. Thesis. Queensland University Rockhampton, Australia.

Keh, H.T., Nguyen, T.T.M. and Ng, H.P. (2007). The effects of entrepreneurial orientation and marketing information on the performance of SMEs. Journal of Business Venturing, 22(4), 592-611.

Keith E. Stanovich., Richard F.West (2000). Individual differences in reasoning: Implications for the rationality debate? *Behavioral and Brain Scienc.* vol. 23, pp. 645–726.

Kerr, A. W., Hall, H. K. and Kozub, S. A.(2002). *Doing Statistics with SPSS,* SAGE Publications, London.

Kristiansen, S., Furoholt, B and Wahid, F. (2003). Internet café entrepreneurs: pioneers in information dissemination in Indonesia. *The International Journal of Entrepreneurship and Innovation.*

Kotler, P, Armstrong, G and Cunningham, PH 2005, *Principles of Marketing,* 5th Canadian edn., Prentice Hall, Toronto, ON.

Kivela, J., Inbakaran, R., and Reece, J. 2000, "Consumer Research in the Restaurant Environment, Part 3: Analysis, Findings and

Conclusions", *International Journal of Contemporary Hospitality Management,* Vol. 12, No. I, pp. 13-30.

Knowles, Ron, and Debbie White (1995). Issues in canadian Small business.Toronto: Harcourt Brace & company Canada.

Locke, Edwin A.; Shaw, Karyll N.; Saari, Lise M.; Latham, Gary P. *Psychological Bulletin*, Vol 90(1), Jul 1981, pp.125-152

Lybaert, N. (*1998*), "The *information* use in an SME: its importance and some elements of influence", Small Business Economics, 10: 171-91. Malaysia, Small and Medium Business Annual Report (2008), Ministry of Finance Malaysia, (MOF).

R. Lawson, and W. Block. 1996. *Economic Freedom of the World, 1975- 1995* (Vancouver: The Fraser Institute).

Pannakarn Leepaiboon (2007). *A Model of Consumer Decision-Making for the Adoption of Thai Food in Victoria, Australia.* Victoria University Melbourne, Australia

Lyles, MA, Baird, IS, Orris, JB and Kuratko, DF (1996) Formalized planning in small business: increasing strategic choices", *Journal of Small Business Management,* April, pp. 38-50.

Laforet, S. (2008). Size, strategic, and market orientation affects on innovation. *Journal of Business Research*, 61(7), pp.753-764.

Li, Y., Zhao, Y., Tan, J. & Liu, Y. (2008). Moderating Effects of Entrepreneurial Orientation on Market Orientation-Performance Linkage: Evidence from Chinese Small Firms. *Journal of Small Business Management*, 46(1), pp.113- 133.

Lazaridis, IT(2004). Capital budgeting practices: a survey in the firms in Cyprus", *Journal of Small Business Management,* vol. 42, no. 4, pp. 427-433.

M. Krishna Moorthy, Annie Tan, Caroline Choo, Chang Sue Wei, Jonathan Tan Yong Ping, and Tan Kah Leong (2012). Study on Factors Affecting the Performance of SMEs in Malaysia, *International Journal of Academic Research in Business and Social Sciences,* April 2012, Vol. 2, No. 4.

Mador, M.(2000) Strategic decision making process research: are entrepreneur and owner managed firms different?, *Journal of Research in Marketing & Entrepreneurship*, vol.2, pp. 215-234.

Mason, L., (2002). *Qualitative Researching,* Sage Publications, Inc.

Megicks, P. and Warnaby, G. (2008). Market orientation and performance in small independent retailers in the UK. *The International Review of Retail, Distribution and Consumer Research*, 18(1), 105-119.

Marwan (2010). *Location decision making processes of internationalizing firms.* Ph.D. Thesis. Curtain University of Technology, Australia.

Mazzarol, T., Volery, T., Doss, N and Thein, V. (1999). Factors influencing small business start ups. International journal of Entrepreneurial Behavior and Research, 5(2): pp.48-63.

Mason, K., and Bequette, J. 1998, "Product Experience and Consumer Product Attribute Inference Accuracy", *Journal of Consumer Marketing,* Vol.15, No.4, pp.343-357.

Mason, Mark (2010). Sample size and Saturation in PhD studies using qualitative interview. Forum: qualitative social research, 11(3).

McDevitt, R., Giapponi, C., & Tromley, C. (2007). A model of ethical decision making: The integration of process and content. *Journal of Business Ethics, 73*, pp. 219-229.

McGee, J.E./Saywerr, O.O. (2003). Uncertainty and information search activities: A study of owner-managers of small high-technology manufacturing firms. *Journal of Small Business Management*, 41 (4), pp. 385-401

McKee (2004). A new approach to uncertainty in business valuation. *The CPA Journal.* vol. 74, pp.46-49.

McCartan-Quinn, D. and Carson, D. (2003). Issues which Impact upon Marketing in the Small Firm. *Small Business Economics,* 21(2), pp.201-231.

Matlay, J 1999, "Employee relations in small firms: a micro-business perspective", *Employee Relations,* vol. 21, no. 3, pp. 285-295.

Marchesnay M. For a dynamic entrepreneurial approach to resources - Jurisdiction. Test praxeology, Les Editions de l'ADREG, 2002.

March, JG and Shapira, Z 1987, 'Managerial perspectives on risk and risk taking', *Management Science,* vol. 33, no. 11, pp. 1404-1418

McMahon, RGP & Holmes, S (1991).Small business financial management practices in North America: a literature review, *Journal of Small Business Management,* April, pp. 19-29.

Mike Simpson and Jo Padmore (2006), Marketing in small and medium sized enterprises, *International Journal of Entrepreneurial Behaviour & Research,* vol. 12 No. 6, pp.361-387

McPherson, M. (2007). A comparison of marketing practices: perspectives from first and second generation UK South Asians. *International Journal of Consumer studies,* 31(2), 174-186.

Monkhouse, E (1995). The role of competitive benchmarking in small to medium- sized enterprises", *Benchmarking for Quality Management Technology,* vol. 2, no. 4, pp. 41-50.

McGee, J.E. (2000) Personal networking activities and venture performance: Lessons from small high technology manufacturing firms. *Association for Small Business and Entrepreneurship.*

McGraw, E., and Roger, A. (2001). Toward the development of a measurement instrument for entrepreneurial motivation. *Journal of Developmental Entrepreneurship,* 6, 189-202

Mackenzie, N and Knipe, S 2006, "Research dilemmas: paradigms, methods and methodology", *Issues in Educational Research,* vol. 16, no. 2, pp. 193-205.

McLennan, W. (1999). *An Introduction to Sample Surveys: A User's Guide,* Australian Bureau of Statistics, Commonwealth of Australia, Canberra

Meziou, F. (1991). Areas of Strength and Weakness in the Adoption of the Marketing Concept by Small Manufacturing Firms. *Journal of Small Business Management,* 29(4), pp.72-78.

Messeghem, K. (2003). Strategic entrepreneurship and managerial activities in SME. *International Small Business Journal 21*(2): 197.

Mike Simpson, M., Padmore, Jo., Taylor, N.J, Hughes.F.(2006) Marketing in small and medium sized enterprises. *International Journal of Entrepreneurial Behaviour & Research.* vol. 12, pp. 361-387

Miles, M. B., and Huberman, A. M. (1984), *Qualitative Data Analysis: A Sourcebook of New Methods,* SAGE Publications, California.

Miles, M. B., & Huberman, A. M. 1994, *Qualitative Data Analysis: An Expanded*

Miller, N., Besser, T. (2005). Exploring decision strategies and evaluations of performance by networked and non-networked small U.S. businesses. *Journal of Developmental Entrepreneurship,* vol.10(2), pp.167-186.

Miller, C.C. & Ireland, R.D.2004, 'Decision making and firm success, *The Academy of management executive,* vol. 18, no. 4, p8.

Mockaitis, A.I., E.Vaiginiene (2006). The internationalization efforts of Lithunian manufacturing firms-strategy or luck?, *Research in International Business and Finance,* 20(1), 111-26.

Megicks, P. and Warnaby, G. (2008). Market orientation and performance in small independent retailers in the UK. *The International Review of Retail, Distribution and Consumer Research,* 18(1), 105-119.

Mintzberg, Raisinghami and Theoret (1976). The structure of unstructured decision process. *Administrative Science Quartley,* vol 21, pp.246-275.

Mintzberg (1990) 'Studying deciding: *Organization Studies,* vol. 11, no. 1, pp. 1-15.

Mintzberg, H and Westley, F 2001, 'Decision making: It's not what you think', *MIT Sloan Management Review,* vol. 42, no. 3, pp. 89-93.

Mohd Sobri Minai, Yusnidah Ibrahim, Law Kuan Kheng (2010), Entrepreneurial Network in Malaysia: Are there any differences across Ethnic Groups?. *Journal of Business and Policy Research Vol. 7. No. 1. April 2012 Special Issue. Pp. 178 – 192*

Nardi, P.M. (2003), *Doing Survey Research: A Guide to Quantitative Methods*, Pearson Education, Boston.

Normah Mohd. Aris (2006). SMEs: Building Blocks For Economic Growth. *National Statistics Conference Department of Statistics*, Malaysia

Noor Hazlina Ahmad and Pi-Shen Seet (2009). A Qualitative Study of SME Owners in Malaysia and Australia. *Asian social science.* Vol 5, no 9.

Nor Hazana Abdullah, Eta Wahab, Alina Shamsuddin (2010). Human Resource Management Practices as Predictorsof Innovation among Johor SMEs. *International conference on science social research (CSSR 2010).* 5-7 December. Kuala Lumpur.

Newton, K. (2001). Small business information needs assessment survey.

Neuman, W. (2003). Social research methods: Qualitative and quantitative approaches.

Neumann, S. and Hadass, M.1980,'DSS and strategic decision', *California management review*, vol.22, no.3, pp.77-84.

Nicholas. C (2004). *The application of TQM within small and medium sized construction related organisations.* Doctoral, Sheffield Hallam University

Oppenheim, A. N. 1986, *Questionnaire Design and Attitude Measurement,* Gower Publishing, Hants.

O'Reilly (1990), 'The use of information in organizational decision making', in L. L. Cummings & B. M. Straw (eds.), *Information and cognition in organizations,* JAI Press Ltd., London, pp. 89-125.

Olafsson (2003). Making decision under uncertainty: Implication for high technology investments. *BT Technology Journal.* Vol.21, pp.170-183.

O'Dwyer, M., Gilmore, A. and Carson, D. (2009). Innovative marketing in SMEs. *European Journal of Marketing*, 43(1/2), pp.46-61.

Oviatt, Benjamin M. and Patricia P. McDougall (2005), "The Internationalization of Entrepreneurship," *Journal of International Business Studies*, Vol. 36, No. 1, pp. 2-8.

Pallant, J. 2002, *SPSS Survival Manual: A Step by Step Guide to Data Analysis Using SPSS for Windows (Version 12)*, Allen & Unwin, NSW.

Pallant, J. 2005, *SPSS Survival Manual: A Step by Step Guide to Data Analysis Using SPSS (2nd Edition)*, Allen & Unwin, NSW.

Patton, M.Q. (1989). Purposeful sampling. In *Qualitative Education Sampling* (p. 1 00- 107). Newbury Park: Sage Publications.

Patton, M. Q. 2002, *Qualitative Research & Evaluation Methods (3rd Edition)*, SAGE Publications, California.

Patton. D, Marlow. S, (2000) "Transactional learning relationships: developing management competencies for effective small firm-stakeholder interactions", Education + Training, Vol. 42 Iss: 4/5, pp.237 – 245

Peterson, R.T. (1989). Small Business Adoption of the Marketing Concept vs. Other Business Strategies. *Journal of Small Business Management*, 27(1), 38-46.

Peel, MJ and Bridge, J (1998). How planning and capital budgeting improve SME performance", *Long Range Planning*, vol. 31, no. 6, pp. 848-856. Peacock, R.W., *Understanding Small Business*, Bookshelf Pubnet, Adelaide

Payne, J.W. (1992).*Behavioral decision research. A constructive processing perspective*. Annual Review of Psychology. V ol 43, pp.87-131.

Payne, A. and Frow, P. (2005). A Strategic Framework for Customer Relationship Management. *Journal of Marketing*, 69(4), pp.167-176.

Payne, G., Kennedy, K., Blair, J., Fottler, M. (2005). Strategic cognitive maps of small business leaders. *Journal of Small Business Strategy*, vol.16(1), pp. 27-40.

Pineda, R.C., Lerner, L.D., Miller, M.C., and Phillips, S.J. (1997). *Which factors influence the information-search activities of small business managers?* ASBE Conference Proceedings.

Pineda, R.C., Lerner, L.D., and Miller, M.C. (2003). Small business managers and the search for information: The costs and benefits of seeking expert advice. *17th Annual USASBE National Conference Proceedings.* Retrieved November 20, 2004 from http://www.sbaer.uca.edu/research/asbe

Rangone, A (1999) 'A Resource-Based Approach to Strategy Analysis in Small- Medium Sized Enterprises', *Small Business Economics,* vol. 12.

Renko, M., Carsrud, A., Brännback, M. and Jalkanen, J. (2005). Building market orientation in biotechnology SMEs: balancing scientific advances. *International Journal of Biotechnology,* 7(4), pp.250-268.

Reynolds, P.L. (2002). The Need for a New Paradigm for Small Business Marketing? – What is Wrong with the Old One? *Journal of Research in Marketing & Entrepreneurship,* 4(3), pp. 191-205.

Riley, TB (2003). International tracking survey report '03: Information management and e-government, Ottawa: Commonwealth centre for electronic governance

Ritchie, R and Brindlely, C 2000, 'Disintermediation, disintegration and risk in the SME global supply chain', *Management Decision,* vol. 38, no. 8, p. 8.

Ritchie, J. and Lewis, J., (2003). *Qualitative Research Practice: A Guide for Social Science Students and Researchers,* SAGE Publications, Inc.

Robbins (2003). *Foundation of management.* Prentice-Hall, Frenchs Forest, NSW.

Robinson, R.B. and Pearce, J.A. (1984), "Research thrusts in small firm strategic planning", *Academy of Management Review,* Vol. 9 No. 1, pp. 128-37.

Roberts, J. H. (2000) Developing new rules for new markets. *Academy of Marketing Science. Journal,* 28, 31-44.

Rowley, C./Benson, J. (eds) (2004): Managing Human Resources in the Asia Pacific Region: Convergence Reconsidered. London: Frank Cass.

Rowntree, D. 1981, *Statistics Without Tears: A Primer for Non-Mathematicians,* Clays, London.

Raffe, S., Sloan, E. L., Vencill, M.P. (1994). *How small businesses learn.* Oakland: Berkeley Planning Associates.

Salimah Mohamed Abdul Hassan, Syamsyul Samsudin, & Yuslizawati Mohd Yusoff (2007). The journey of Female SMEs: Malaysia evidence. *Proceeding of 4th SMEs in a Global Economy International Conference.* Shah Alam: UPENA.

Sander Wennekers (2005). Entrepreneurship, small business and economic growth, *Journal of Small Business and Enterprise Development,* vol.11(1).pp. pp.140- 149

Sashittal, H.C. and Jassawalla, A.R. (2001). Marketing Implementation in Smaller Organizations: Definition, Framework, and Propositional Inventory. *Journal of the Academy of Marketing Science,* 29(1), pp.50-69.

Shukor Omar (2006). *Malay Business.* Subang Jaya: Pelanduk Publications.

Sexton, D.L. (1997). Entrepreneurship research needs and issues. In D.K. Sexton & R.W. Smilor (Eds.). *Entrepreneurship 2000,* (pp. 401-408). Chicago: Upstart Publishing Co.

Shoa. A (2005). Decision waves;consumer decision in today's complex world. *European Journal of marketing,* 39(1/2), pp.216-230.

Shoa. A(2006). Marketing Research: An Aid to Decision Making, Atomic Dog; 3 edition (December 11, 2006)

Schoemaker, J. H., and Russo, J. E. (1993). A pyramid of decision approaches. *California Management Review, 36*(1), 9–31.

Simon (1997), *Administrative behaviour: A study of decision-making processes in administrative organizations,* (4th edn.), The Free Press, New York.

Simons and Thompson, BM 1998, 'Strategic determinants: The context of managerial decision making', *Journal of Managerial Psychology*, vol. 13, no. 1,2, pp. 7- 21.

Simon (1977). Rational decision making in business organization. *American Economic Review*, vol. 69, pp.493-513.

Simpson, M., Padmore, J., Taylor, N. and Frecknall-Hughes, J. (2006). Marketing in small and medium sized enterprises. *International Journal of Entrepreneurial Behaviour & Research*, 12(6), pp.361-387.

Siu, W. and Kirby, D.A. (1998). Approaches to small firm marketing. A Critique. *European Journal of Marketing*, 32(1/2), pp.40-60.

Spilling, O., and berg, N.(2000). Gender and Small Business Managemnet: The case of Norway in the 1990s. *International small business journal*, vol.18, no 2, pp.38- 59.

Stokes, D. (2000). Entrepreneurial marketing: a conceptualisation from qualitative research. *Qualitative Market Research: An International Journal*, 3(1), pp.47- 54.

Stokes, D. (2000). Putting Entrepreneurship into Marketing: The Processes of Entrepreneurial Marketing. *Journal of Research in Marketing & Entrepreneurship*, 2(1), pp.1-16.

Stonehouse, G & Pemberton, J 2002, "Strategic planning in SMEs: some empirical findings", *Management Decision*, vol. 40, no. 9, pp. 853-861.

Sotrines, F.A. (1984). *An approach to assessing business continuing education needs of small business owner/managers.* Unpublished doctoral dissertation, Kansas State University, Manhattan.

Schiffrnan, L., Bednall, D., Cowley, E., Cass, A. O., Watson, J., and Kanuk, L. 2001, *Consumer Behaviour (2nd Edition),* An imprint of Pearson Education, Australia.

Sekaran, U. 2000, *Research Methods for Business: A Skill-Building Approach (3rd Edition),* John Wiley and Sons, New York

Simon. H.A (1995). *A behavioral model of Rational choice,* Quarterly Journal of Economics, 69(1), pp. 99-118.

SMIDEC (2002). SMI Development Plan (2001–2005), *Percetakan Nasional Malaysia Berhad*, Kuala Lumpur

Stokes, D. (2000). Entrepreneurial marketing: a conceptualisation from qualitative research. *Qualitative Market Research: An International Journal*, 3(1), pp. 47-54.

Stokes, D. (2000). Putting Entrepreneurship into Marketing: The Processes of Entrepreneurial Marketing. *Journal of Research in Marketing & Entrepreneurship*, 2(1), pp. 1-16.

Sekaran, U. 2000, Research Methods for Business: A Skill-Building Approach (3rd Edition), John Wiley & Sons, New York.

United Parcel Services (2005). UPS Reveals Asia Business Monitor Survey Findings, online available at http://www.ups.com

Shapira (1994). *Risk taking: a managerial perspective.* Russel sage Foundation, New York. Sternberg, R. J. (2004). Successful intelligence as a basis for entrepreneurship. *Journal of business venturing*, Vol. 19, 189–201.

Syahira Hamidon (2009). *The development of Malay Entrepreneurship in Malaysia.* Ph.D. Thesis. Massey University, Auckland, New Zealand.

Wai-Sum Siu / Heinz Klandt: The climate for Entrepreneurship: A comparative study of China and Hong Kong. In. *Academy of Entrepreneurship Journal*, 2000, Volume 6, No. 2, pp. 38-49.

Tabachnick, B. G., and Fidell, L. S. 2001, *Using Multivariate Statistics (4th Edition)*, Harper Collins, New York.

Taylor, D.W. and Thorpe, R. (2004) 'Entrepreneurial Learning:a process of co- participation', *Journal of Small Business and Enterprise Development*, February, vol 11 No 2 pp. 203-211.

Tashakkori, A., and Teddlie, C. 1998, *Mixed Methodology: Combining Qualitative and Quantitative Approaches,* SAGE Publications, Califomia.

Tesch, R. 1990, *Qualitative Research: Analysis Types and Software Tools,* The Falmer Press, London

Ting (2004). "SMEs in Malaysia: Pivot points for Change", online available at http://www.mca.org.my.

Turner, B. A. (2002). *Understanding the three dimensions of decision-making as a means of transforming the organization.* (Doctoral Dissertation, University of Phoenix, 2002) Torres, O. SMEs, Paris, 1999

Thompson, J.L (2004). The facet of the entrepreneur. Identifying entrepreneurial potential. Management Deciison,42(2), pp. 243-258.

Ucbasaran, D.(2008). Habitual Entrepreneurs, Foundations and Trends in Entrepreneurship, now Publisher Inc, Hanover.

Vorhies, G.W. (1998). An investigation of the factors leading to the development of marketing capabilities and organizational effectiveness. *Journal of Strategic Marketing,* 6(1), 3-23.

Varraut, N. Vision for strategic: An application to dirigeantpropriétaire of SMEs in Economies and Societies, Scienc in Management, No. 26-2, 1999.

Veitch, K & Smith, EH 2000, "The evaluation of customer service performance and the small business – a case study within the packaging supply chain", in Proceedings from the 3rd SMESME International Conference, Coventry University, Coventry, pp. 216-221.

Wasilczuck, J.(2000), Advantageous Competence of owner manager to grow the firm in Poland. *Journal of small business management,* vol.38.no.2.

Frederick E. Webster, Jr.(1992) The Changing Role of Marketing in the Corporation, *Journal of Marketing* Vol. 56, No. 4 (Oct., 1992), pp. 1-17

Walker, W. and Brown, A. (2004) What success factors are important to small business owners?", *International Small Business Journal,* Vol. 22(6), pp. 577-594.

Weiss, A., Lurie, N., & MacInnis, D. (2008). *Listening to strangers: Whose responses are valuable, how valuable are they, and why?* Journal of Marketing Research, vol. 45(4), p.p 425-436.

Wallis, E. and Winterton, J. (2002) 'A new social partnership in steel? Community learning and union renewal in the UK steel and metal sector', in L. Montanheiro, S. Beger and G. Skomsoy (Eds) *Public and Private Sector Partnerships: Exploring Cooperation*, Sheffield: PAVIC Publications, 505- 516.

Williams, V. (1999). E-commerce: Small businesses venture online. *Office of Advocacy US Small Business Administration*. Washington, DC: US Government Printing Office. Retrieved from http://www.sba.gov/advo

Wolcott, H. F. (1994). *Transforming Qualitative Data: Description, Analysis, and Interpretation,* SAGE Publications, Califomia.

Wong (1995). The impact of management training and development on SMEs. *International small business journal,*13, pp.23-34.

Woods, A and Joyce, P (2003).Owner-managers and the practice of strategic management", *International Small Business Journal,* vol. 21, no. 2, pp. 181- 195.

Wolcott, H. F. 2001, *Writing Up Qualitation Research,* SAGE Publications, California.

Young, M., Wyman, S.M., & Brenner, C.T. (1999). *Assessment of small business perception of needed information and assistance.* ASBE Conference Proceedings

Zikmund, W. G. 2000, *Business Research Methods (6th Edition),* The Dryden Press, Harcourt College Publishers, Oriando, FL.

Zikmund, WG 2003, *Business Research Methods*, (7th edn.), The Dryden Press, Fort Worth, TX.

APPENDIX A

Semi-Structured Questions:

A list of questions follow that will be used as a guideline to conduct the qualitative research of the small to medium sized enterprise.

Section 1: Decision method

The following section will ask the respondent the process of making marketing decision.

- In your word, what is your understanding of marketing decision making process?
- What is the approach has been used in the process?

Section 2: Source of information

The following section will ask the source of information use in the process.

- What kinds of sources of information do you use in the marketing decision -making process?

Section 3: Driving Factor

The following section will ask the respondent the factor influencing the approach of the decision.

- What is the factor influence the decision approach?

Section 4: Decision outcome

The following section will ask respondent perception on the outcome of the process.
- What is the result of your decision?
- Have satisfied with the approach being use in the process?

Section 5

The following questions will be asked to all participants;

1. Please state your job title.
2. How long have you worked for this company?
3. Please describe the role of your position.
4. How long have you worked in this role?

Interview:
Name of Interviewee:
Date of Interview:
Time of Interview:
Length of Interview:

SECTION A

Decision Method

Instruction:

Please respond to the questions based on your personal opinion and knowledge. Mark your responses with X in one box only.

1. **What decision-making method do you most frequently use in marketing?**

   i.   Formal   ☐

   ii. Informal   ☐

   iii. Both Formal & Informal   ☐

   iv. Strategic Decision Making   ☐

   v.   Other (Please specify) _____ ☐

SECTION B

Information Factor

Instruction:

Please respond to the questions based on your personal opinion and knowledge. Mark your responses with X in the box.

2. **What kinds of sources of information do you use in the marketing decision - making process? Use the following list to prompt for resources if needed.**

		Strongly unlikely	Unlikely	Neutral	Likely	Strongly likely
		1	2	3	4	5
i.	Past experience	☐	☐	☐	☐	☐
ii.	Formal education	☐	☐	☐	☐	☐
iii.	Other business managers (similar business, competitors)	☐	☐	☐	☐	☐
iv.	Friends/ social networks	☐	☐	☐	☐	☐
v.	Your Suppliers	☐	☐	☐	☐	☐
vi.	Your Customers	☐	☐	☐	☐	☐
vii.	Your Family	☐	☐	☐	☐	☐

Hairul Rizad and Abu Bakar

i.	Media (including TV, newspapers, and magazines, etc)	☐	☐	☐	☐	☐
ii.	The Internet	☐	☐	☐	☐	☐
iii.	External private sector consultants (banker, accountant, lawyer)	☐	☐	☐	☐	☐
iv.	Banks or other financial institutions	☐	☐	☐	☐	☐
v.	Seminars/conference/ workshops	☐	☐	☐	☐	☐
vi.	Marketing/Trade Exhibition	☐	☐	☐	☐	☐
vii.	Industry or SMEs associations	☐	☐	☐	☐	☐
viii.	Government (SME's corp., Matrade, etc)	☐	☐	☐	☐	☐

3. **If you do not agree with the above items suggested in question two (2), please describe your own experience.**

_____

_____

SECTION C

Driving factors

Instruction:

Please respond to the questions based on your personal opinion and knowledge. Mark your responses with X in one box only.

4. **To what extent do you think the following factors are important to the effectiveness for your marketing decision making process?**

		Not at all	To small extent	To some extent	To large extent	To a very large extent
		1	2	3	4	5
i.	Personal vision	☐	☐	☐	☐	☐
ii.	Personal competency	☐	☐	☐	☐	☐
iii.	Long term business relationship	☐	☐	☐	☐	☐
iv.	Goal setting	☐	☐	☐	☐	☐
v.	Personal and lifestyle consideration	☐	☐	☐	☐	☐

Hairul Rizad and Abu Bakar

vi.	Ethical and social consideration	☐	☐	☐	☐	☐
vii.	Personal experience	☐	☐	☐	☐	☐
viii.	Financial return (Profit margin)	☐	☐	☐	☐	☐
ix.	Company financial capability	☐	☐	☐	☐	☐
x.	Market size	☐	☐	☐	☐	☐
xi.	Risk size	☐	☐	☐	☐	☐
xii.	Size of the company	☐	☐	☐	☐	☐
xiii.	Business association i.e. SME's association	☐	☐	☐	☐	☐

5. **If you do not agree with the above items suggested in question four (4), please describe your own experience.**

_____

_____

_____

_____

_____

SECTION D

Decision outcome

Instruction:

Please respond to the questions based on your personal opinion and knowledge. Mark your responses with X in one box only.

6. What is the result of your decision?

		strongly disagree	Disagree	Neutral	Agree	Strongly agree
		1	2	3	4	5
i	We are very satisfied, everything went as planned(i.e. goals are reached)	☐	☐	☐	☐	☐
ii	We are satisfied, even though we experienced minor complications	☐	☐	☐	☐	☐
iii	Nothing has changed, no improvements are seen	☐	☐	☐	☐	☐
iv	We are not satisfied, our goals have not been fulfilled	☐	☐	☐	☐	☐

Hairul Rizad and Abu Bakar

SECTION E

Respondents' Background

Instruction:

For each statement, please mark your response with X in one box only.

7. **Present designation in company**

   i.   Managing Director   ☐
   ii.   Chief Executive Officer   ☐
   iii. General Manager   ☐
   iv.   Senior Manager   ☐
   v.   (Please specify)_____   ☐

8. **Length of time working in your designated position**

   i.   Less than 1 years   ☐
   ii.   Between 1 - 3 years   ☐
   iii. Between 3 - 4 years   ☐
   iv.   More than 5 Years   ☐

9. **Age**

   i.   Less than 40 years old   ☐
   ii.   Between 40 and 55 years old   ☐
   iii. Above 55 years old   ☐

10. Length of time spent working in the company

i. Less than 5 years ☐

ii. 5 to 10 years ☐

iii. 11 to 20 years ☐

iv. More than 20 years ☐

11. Gender

i. Male ☐

ii. Female ☐

12. Race

i. Malay ☐

ii. Chinese ☐

iii. Indian ☐

iv. Other (Please specify)_____ ☐

13. Highest education level

i. High School ☐

ii. Diploma ☐

iii. Bachelor's Degree ☐

iv. Master's Degree ☐

v. PhD ☐

vi. Other (Please specify)_____ ☐

14. Categories which best describe your main business activities

i. Agriculture ☐

ii. Automotive ☐

iii. Building & Construction ☐

iv.	Chemicals	☐
v.	Electrical & Electronic	☐
vi.	Education & Training	☐
vii	Food & Beverages	☐
viii	Furniture	☐
ix	ICT	☐
x	Industrial Equipment	☐
xi	Logistics	☐
xii	Machinery & Engineering	☐
xiii	Manufacturing	☐
xiv	Marine	☐
xv	Office Product & Services	☐
xvi	Oil & Gas	☐
xvii	Packaging	☐
xviii	Plastic	☐
xix	Printing	☐
xx	Retail & Wholesale	☐
xxi	Rubber	☐
xxii	Textile & Apparel	☐
xxiii	Timber	☐
xxiv	Trading	☐
xxv	Transport	☐

15. Annual sales turnover of your business

i.	Less than MYR 250,000	☐
ii.	MYR 200,000 - MYR 1 million	☐
iii.	MYR 1 million - MYR 5 million	☐
iv.	MYR 5 million - MYR 10 million	☐
v.	More than MYR 10 million	☐

16. Number of employees

i.	Less than 5	☐
ii.	Between 5 to 20	☐
iii.	Between 21 to 50	☐
iv.	Between 51 to 100	☐
v.	More than 100	☐

17. Where would you place your business in the following stages of business development?

i.	Start up/Early formation stage (e.g. just getting started)	☐
ii.	Early Growth (e.g. experience growth in sales, but still a new business)	☐
iii.	Later growth (e.g. sales growth is slowing, due to increased competition)	☐
iv.	Stability(e.g. sales have somewhat leveled off, but management is well established)	☐
v.	Other (Please specify)_____	☐

Thank you for your time and cooperation in completing this questionnaire

Printed in the United States
By Bookmasters